Word Master

Seeing and Using Words

LEVEL 6

Lessons 1- 30

Series Designer
Philip J. Solimene

Editors
Janice Colby Solimene
Laura Solimene

Consultant
Douglas P. Barnard, Ed.D

Author
David L. Bacon

EDCON PUBLISHING GROUP
www.edconpublishing.com

30 Montauk Blvd. Oakdale NY 11769
info@edconpublishing.com
www.edconpublishing.com
1-888-553-3266 Fax 1-888-518-1564

Printed in U.S.A.
ISBN# 0-931334-32-2

CONTENTS

INTRODUCTION

What do you do when you see a word you do not know? Do you use a dictionary to learn its meaning, do you look at the parts of the word to find a "root" word, or do you try to understand the word's meaning from its context?

New words can be learned in different ways. One good way to understand the meaning of a word is to understand what it means in the sentence or paragraph where it is used. To do this, you must understand the meaning of the sentence or paragraph you are reading.

However, understanding a word in context will not always teach you all you should know about the word. A dictionary will be needed for you to learn how to pronounce the word and to learn the word's meaning or meanings.

This book will help you to:

1. Learn the use of context clues
2. Learn the use of a dictionary
3. Learn the different forms of words

THE WAY TO USE THIS BOOK

Look at the CONTENTS page (page iii). The large black type will show you the four main parts of the book: SEQUENCE 6-1 through SEQUENCE 6-30, EXERCISE G, ANSWER KEY, and PROGRESS CHART.

Then, turn to SEQUENCE 6-1. Look at the four pages that make up SEQUENCE 6-1. Every sequence in the book is similar. Every sequence has six sections that follow one another:

A Writing the Words
B Using Context Clues
C Checking the Meaning
D Completing the Sentences
E Using the Skill
F Supplementary Writing Exercise

A seventh section

G Sentences for Spelling Exercise

Use CONTENTS page to locate sentences for Spelling Exercise.

Instructions for each of these sections are on the next page.
Your teacher will provide instruction in rules for recognizing and spelling different forms of words.

A WRITING THE WORDS

1. Write the word you see to the left of the blank lines, beginning with number 1.
2. Say each word after you write it.
3. Follow the instructions for part B of this section.

B USING CONTEXT CLUES

1. At the top of the page are entries as they appear in a dictionary. Read the entries and their meanings. All the words will be used in some of the exercises. If you have trouble pronouncing a word, use the Pronunciation Key on the inside of the back cover of this book.
2. Follow the instructions for the exercise. When you have completed the exercise, check your answers with the Answer Key.

C CHECKING THE MEANING

Follow the instructions for the exercise. When you have completed the exercise, check your answers with the Answer Key.

D COMPLETING THE SENTENCES

Follow the instructions for the exercise. When you have completed the exercise, check your answers with the Answer Key. Enter your score on the Progress Chart.

E USING THE SKILL

Follow the instructions for the exercise. When you have completed the exercise, check your answers with the Answer Key. Enter your score on the Progress Chart.

F SUPPLEMENTARY WRITING EXERCISE

Follow the instructions for the exercise. There is no Answer Key for this exercise. Your teacher will check your work.

G SENTENCES FOR SPELLING EXERCISE

1. Each sentence in this exercise contains one of your new words. The new words are underlined.
2. Two or three days after you have completed the four pages of exercises for one sequence, your teacher may want to know how well you have learned the new words. The teacher may pronounce the new word, then read the sentence that uses the word, then pronounce the word again.
3. You are to write the word on a separate sheet of paper. Enter your score on the Progress Chart. Then correct any mistakes you made.
4. You might be asked to use the sentences in this exercise to give a spelling test to someone else.

A WRITING THE WORDS

A. Write these words on the blank lines.
Then say each word.

Write

		Write
submarine	1.	______
subtract	2.	______
exit	3.	______
descend	4.	______
except	5.	______
deposit	6.	______
describe	7.	______
subdivision	8.	______
exhaust	9.	______
derive	10.	______

B. Each word begins with a prefix.
Write the prefix for each word.

1. ______
2. ______
3. ______
4. ______
5. ______
6. ______
7. ______
8. ______
9. ______
10. ______

THESE PREFIXES HAVE MEANINGS THAT GIVE **DIRECTION.**

de - *prefix* [ME, fr. OF *de-, des-*, partly fr. L *de-* from, down, away (fr. *de*) and partly fr. L *dis-*: L *de* akin to OIr *di* from, OE *to* to – more at TO, DIS-] **1 a** : do the opposite of <*de*vitalize> <*de*activate> **b** : reverse of <*de*-emphasis> **2 a** : remove (a specified thing) from <*de*louse> <*de*hydrogenate> **b** : remove from (a specified thing) <*de*throne> **3** : reduce <*de*value> **4** : something derived from (a specified thing) <*de*compound> : derived from something (of a specified nature) <*de*nominative> **5** : get off of (a specified thing) <*de*train> **6** : having a molecule characterized by the removal of one or more atoms (of a specified element) <*de*oxy>

[1]**ex-** \ e *also occurs in this prefix where only* i *is shown below (as in "express") and* ks *sometimes occurs where only* gz *is shown (as in "exact")* \ *prefix* [ME, fr. OF & L; OF, fr. L (also, intensive prefix), fr. *ex* out of, from; akin to Gk *ex-* out of, from OSlav *iz*] **1** : out of : outside <*ex*clave> **2** : not (*ex*stipulate> **3** : \ (ˌ)eks, ˈeks\ [ME, fr. LL, fr. L] : former <*ex*-president> <*ex*-child actor>
[2]**ex** \ (ˌ)eks \ *prep* [L] **1 a** : out of : FROM (as from a specified place or source) <*ex*factory> **b** : a function word used by breeders to identify the dam of an animal <a promising calf by Eric XVI ~ Heatherbell> **2** : free from : WITHOUT as **a** : without an indicated value or right – used esp. of securities **b** : free of charges precedent to removal from the specified place with purchaser to provide means of subsequent transportation <~ dock>
[3]**ex** /ˈeks / *n* : the letter *x*
[4]**ex** *abbr* **1** example **2** exchange **3** executive **4** express **5** extra
Ex *abbr* Exodus

sub- *prefix* [ME, fr. L, under, below, secretly, from below, up, near, fr. *sub* under, close to – more at UP] **1** : under : beneath : below <*sub*soil> **2 a** : subordinate : secondary : next lower than or inferior to <*sub*station> <*sub*editor> **b** : subordinate portion of : subdivision of <*sub*committee> <*sub*species> **c** : with repetition (as of a process) so as to form, stress, or deal with subordinate parts of relations <*sub*let> <*sub*contract> **3 a** : less than completely, perfectly, or normally : somewhat <*sub*dominant> <*sub*ovate> **b** : (1) : containing less than the usual or normal amount of (such) an element or radical <*sub*oxide> (2) : basic – in names of salts <*sub*acetate> **4 a** : almost : nearly <*sub*erect> **b** : falling nearly in the category of and often adjoining : bordering upon <*sub*arctic>

B USING CONTEXT CLUES

Place an X in front of each correct answer. The word may be used correctly in one or both of the sentences.

1. A <u>submarine</u>
   ___a. goes under the water.
   ___b. goes down into the water.

2. When you <u>describe</u> someone on paper,
   ___a. you write down things about that person.
   ___b. you resemble that person.

3. When you <u>subtract</u>,
   ___a. you add numbers to numbers.
   ___b. you take numbers from numbers.

4. An <u>exit</u> sign is
   ___a. a way in.
   ___b. a way out.

5. The man will <u>descend</u> the ladder means
   ___a. the man will go up the ladder.
   ___b. the man will go down the ladder.

Check your answers with the Key on page 137.

C CHECKING THE MEANING

Read the words in the boxes. Choose the word that best completes the sentence under them. Write that word on the line. Then complete the next sentence by placing an X in front of the correct answer.

1. | except | | exit |

We walked toward the ________________.
This sentence means
___a. we walked to our seat.
___b. we walked to the entrance.
___c. we walked to the way out.

2. | deposit | | describe |

The writer will ________________ the actor.
This sentence means
___a. the writer will write the play.
___b. the writer will speak the lines.
___c. the writer will write about the actor.

3. | subtract | | subdivision |

In math, students ________________ numbers.
This sentence means
___a. students add numbers.
___b. students take away numbers.
___c. students leave numbers as they are.

4. | exhaust | | except |

All the students, ________________ for Bill, went to the game.
This sentence means
___a. all the students went to the game.
___b. everyone but Bill went to the game.
___c. no students went to the game.

5. | derive | | descend |

The circus performer will ________________ the rope.
This sentence means
___a. the performer will climb the rope.
___b. the performer will stay on the rope.
___c. the performer will come down the rope.

Check your answers with the Key on page 137.

D COMPLETING THE SENTENCES

Choose a word from the box that best completes each sentence. Write it on the line.

except	derive	deposit	descend
subdivision	exhaust	subtract	describe

1. We will ________________ our money in the bank.
2. The house was located in a small _________________________.
3. Most people ________________ satisfaction from work.
4. All the children will go to the show ________________ John; he has an appointment.
5. The window fan will ________________ the stale air from the room.

Check your answers with the Key on page 137.

E USING THE SKILL

Underline the word that best completes each sentence.

1. The man made his way to the (except, exit).
2. The book will (descend, describe) the characters.
3. Jenny (deposits, derives) a lot of pleasure from her job.
4. When you (deposit, subtract), you take numbers away from numbers.
5. A long trip can (derive, exhaust) you.

Check your answers with the Key on page 137.

F SUPPLEMENTARY WRITING EXERCISE

The prefixes that were taught in this lesson are:

ex-	sub-	de-

Write sentences in which you use each of the prefixes in a word in the sentence.

1. ____
2. ____
3. ____

A WRITING THE WORDS

A. Write these words on the blank lines.
Then say each word.

Write

incomplete	1. ____________
uncertain	2. ____________
invisible	3. ____________
nonsense	4. ____________
independent	5. ____________
uncommon	6. ____________
unconscious	7. ____________
nonliving	8. ____________
nonfiction	9. ____________
unusual	10. ____________

B. Each word begins with a prefix.
Write the prefix for each word.

1. ____________
2. ____________
3. ____________
4. ____________
5. ____________
6. ____________
7. ____________
8. ____________
9. ____________
10. ____________

EACH OF THESE PREFIXES HAS THE MEANING OF **NOT**.

SEQUENCE 6-2

[1]**in-** *or* **il-** *or* **im-** *or* **ir-** *prefix* [ME, fr. MF, fr. L; akin to OE *un-* : not : NON-, UN- – usu. *il-* before *l* <*il*logical> and *im-* before *b, m,* or *p* <*im*balance> <*im*moral> <*im*practical> and *ir-* before *r* <*ir*reducible> and *in-* before other sounds <*in*conclusive>

[2]**in-** *or* **il-** *or* **im-** *or* **ir-** *prefix* [ME, fr. MF, fr. L, fr. *in* in, into] **1** : in : within : into : toward : on <*il*luviation> <*im*mingle> <*ir*radiance> – usu. *il-* before *l, im-* before *b, m,* or *p, ir-* before *r,* and *in-* before other sounds **2** : EN- <*im*brute> <*im*peril> <*in*spirit>

non- \ (ˈ) nän *also,* nən *or* ˈnən *before* ˈ*-stressed syllable,* ˌnän also, ˌnən, *before* ˌ*-stressed or unstressed syllable; the variant with e is also to be understood at pronounced entries, where it is not shown* \ *prefix* [ME, fr. MF, fr. L *non* not, fr. OL *noenum,* fr. *ne-* not + *oinom,* neut. of *oinos* one – more at NO, ONE] **1** : not : reverse of : absence of **2** : of little or no consequence : unimportant : worthless : <*non*issues> <*non*system> **3** : lacking the usual characteristics of the thing specified <*non*celebration> <*non*theater>

un- *prefix* [ME, fr. OE *un-* *on-*, alter, of *and-* against – more at ANTE-] **1** : do the opposite of : reverse (a specified action) : DE- la, DIS- la – in verbs formed from verbs <*un*bend> <*un*dress> <*un*fold> **2** **a** : deprive of : remove (a specified thing) from : remove – in verbs formed from nouns <*un*frock> <*un*sex> **b** : release from : free from – in verbs formed from nouns <*un*hand> **c** : remove from : extract from : bring out of – in verbs formed from nouns <*un*bosom> **d** : cause to cease to be – in verbs formed from nouns <*un*man> 3 : completely <*un*loose>

B USING CONTEXT CLUES

Place an X in front of each correct answer. The word may be used correctly in one or both of the sentences.

1. An assignment that is <u>incomplete</u> is
   ___a. finished.
   ___b. not finished.

2. A person that is <u>uncertain</u>
   ___a. makes decisions easily.
   ___b. hesitates in making decisions.

3. To say that something is <u>invisible</u>
   ___a. is to not see it.
   ___b. is to see it clearly.

4. A <u>nonsense</u> verse
   ___a. makes sense.
   ___b. makes no sense.

5. When students are <u>independent</u>
   ___a. they depend on the teacher for help.
   ___b. they do not depend on the teacher for help.

Check your answers with the Key on page 137.

C CHECKING THE MEANING

Read the words in the boxes. Choose the word that best completes the sentence under them. Write that word on the line. Then complete the next sentence by placing an X in front of the correct answer.

1. incomplete | uncertain

The student was ______________________________ about the assignment.
This sentence means
___a. the student did not understand the assignment.
___b. the student understood the assignment.
___c. the student was unhappy about the assignment.

2. uncommon | unconscious

Igloos are ______________________________ in the tropics.
This sentence means
___a. igloos are often seen in the tropics.
___b. igloos are not seen in the tropics.
___c. igloos are welcome in the tropics.

3. independent | invisible

The boy was ______________________________ and earned his own money.
This sentence means
___a. the boy needed support.
___b. the boy did not need support.
___c. the boy earned enough to support his parents.

4. nonsense | nonliving

The man's answer to the question was ______________________________.
This sentence means
___a. the man's answer made sense.
___b. the man's answer made good sense.
___c. the man's answer made no sense.

5. nonfiction | unusual

Sightings of UFOs are ______________________________ happenings.
This sentence means
___a. UFOs are ordinary.
___b. UFOs are not ordinary.
___c. UFOs are seen often.

Check your answers with the Key on page 137.

D COMPLETING THE SENTENCES

Choose a word from the box that best completes each sentence. Write it on the line.

unusual	uncertain	uncommon	invisible
unconscious	nonfiction	independent	incomplete

1. The ballplayer became ________________________ after the ball hit him in the head.
2. When glass is clean, it sometimes appears to be ________________________.
3. Books that tell true stories are called ________________________
4. The dog was ________________________ about the way to get back home.
5. The farmer wishes to remain ____________________and will not ask the government for help.

Check your answers with the Key on page 137.

E USING THE SKILL

Underline the word that best completes each sentence.

1. A dictionary may give an (uncommon, unconscious) meaning for a word.
2. Some of the stories in that book are (invisible, nonfiction).
3. I find (unusual, uncertain) stories very interesting.
4. Minerals are (nonfiction, nonliving) substances.
5. A good laugh can sometimes be the result of pure (nonfiction, nonsense).

Check your answers with the Key on page 137.

F SUPPLEMENTARY WRITING EXERCISE

The prefixes that were taught in this lesson are:

un-	non-	in-

Write sentences in which you use each of the prefixes in a word in the sentence.

1. ____
2. ____
3. ____

A WRITING THE WORDS

A. Write these words on the blank lines.
Then say each word.

Write

circumnavigate	1. ______
protect	2. ______
perceive	3. ______
progress	4. ______
circumference	5. ______
circumstances	6. ______
project	7. ______
perform	8. ______
percolate	9. ______
program	10. ______

B. Each word begins with a prefix.
Write the prefix for each word.

1. ______
2. ______
3. ______
4. ______
5. ______
6. ______
7. ______
8. ______
9. ______
10. ______

THESE PREFIXES HAVE MEANINGS THAT GIVE **DIRECTION**.

SEQUENCE 6-3

circum- *prefix* [OF or L; OF, fr. L, fr. *circum*, fr. *circus* circle – more at CIRCLE] : around : about <*circum*polar>

per- *prefix* [L, through, throughout, thoroughly, to destruction, fr. *per*] **1** : throughout : thoroughly <*per*chlorinate> **2 a** : containing the largest possible or a relatively large proportion of a (specified) chemical element <*per*chloride> **b** : containing an element in its highest or a high oxidation state <*per*-chloric acid>

[1]**pro-** *prefix* [ME, fr. OF, fr. L, fr. Gk, before, forward, forth, for, fr. *pro* – more at FOR] **1 a** : earlier than : prior to : before <*pro*thalamion> **b** : rudimentary : PROT. <*pro*nucleus> **2 a** : located in front of or at the front of : anterior to <*pro*cephalic> <*pro*ventriculus> **b** : front : anterior <*pro*thorax> **3** : projecting <*pro*gnathous>

[2]**pro-** *prefix* [L *pro* in front of, before, for – more at FOR] **1** : taking the place of : substituting for <*pro*-cathedral> <*pro*caine> **2** : favoring : supporting : championing <*pro*-American>

B USING CONTEXT CLUES

Place an X in front of each correct answer. The word may be used correctly in one or both of the sentences.

1. To circumnavigate is to
   ___a. go around the world.
   ___b. go around the lake.

2. To protect people is to
   ___a. harm them.
   ___b. keep them from harm.

3. To perceive a solution to a problem is to
   ___a. know the solution.
   ___b. see through the problem to a solution.

4. Progress means
   ___a. to move forward.
   ___b. to move backward.

5. To measure the circumference of a circle is to
   ___a. measure through the circle.
   ___b. measure the distance around the circle.

Check your answers with the Key on page 137.

C CHECKING THE MEANING

Read the words in the boxes. Choose the word that best completes the sentence under them. Write that word on the line. Then complete the next sentence by placing an X in front of the correct answer.

1. circumstances | circumference

The ________________________ surrounding the crime were well known.
This sentence means
___a. the facts of the crime were known.
___b. the facts of the crime were not known.
___c. no crime was committed.

2. project | progress

Much ________________________ was made on the new house.
This sentence means
___a. the house was being built.
___b. the house was not being built.
___c. the house was completely built.

3. perform | percolate

The water will ________________________ in the coffee pot.
This sentence means
___a. the water will drip through small holes.
___b. the water will not drip through small holes.
___c. the water will not boil in the pot.

4. perceive | project

I ________________________ that my brother is mad at me.
This sentence means
___a. I understand that my brother is mad at me.
___b. I wonder if my brother is mad at me.
___c. I am angry with my brother.

5. program | project

If we plant the tree too close to the lake, it will ________________________ over the lake.
This sentence means
___a. the tree will grow under the lake.
___b. the tree will die.
___c. the tree will grow out over the lake.

Check your answers with the Key on page 137.

D COMPLETING THE SENTENCES

Choose a word from the box that best completes each sentence. Write it on the line.

perceive	protect	percolate	circumference
progress	program	perform	circumstances

1. The ______________________ of the ball is 16 inches.
2. "Tim, I ______________________ that you're not doing well in school," said Tim's dad.
3. Pete quickly picked up his cat to ______________________ it from the stray dog.
4. Samantha made a lot of ______________________ in school this year.
5. The ______________________ surrounding the crime were not known.

Check your answers with the Key on page 137.

E USING THE SKILL

Underline the word that best completes each sentence.

1. I cannot (progress, perceive) a solution to the riddle.
2. The young sailor wanted to (circumference, circumnavigate) the world.
3. Much (project, progress) was being made on the repair of the damaged boat.
4. The actors will (protect, perform) for the audience.
5. Let the coffee (project, percolate) for six minutes.

Check your answers with the Key on page 137.

F SUPPLEMENTARY WRITING EXERCISE

The prefixes that were taught in this lesson are:

circum-	per-	pro-

Write sentences in which you use each of the prefixes in a word in the sentence.

1. ____
2. ____
3. ____

A WRITING THE WORDS

A. Write these words on the blank lines.
Then say each word.

Write

postscript	1. ______
postpone	2. ______
predict	3. ______
reflect	4. ______
precede	5. ______
prevent	6. ______
rebuilt	7. ______
recall	8. ______
remember	9. ______
postwar	10. ______

B. Each word begins with a prefix.
Write the prefix for each word.

1. ______
2. ______
3. ______
4. ______
5. ______
6. ______
7. ______
8. ______
9. ______
10. ______

THESE PREFIXES HAVE MEANINGS THAT RELATE TO **TIME**.

SEQUENCE 6-4

post- *prefix* [ME, fr. L, fr. *post*: akin to Skt *paśca* behind, after, Gk *apo* away from – more at OF] **1 a** : after : subsequent : later <*post*date> **b** : behind : posterior : following after <*post*lude> <*post*consonantal> **2 a** : subsequent to : later than <*post*operative> <*post*-Pleistocene> **b** : posterior to <*post*orbital>

pre- *prefix* [ME, fr. OF & L; OF, fr. L *prae-*, fr. *prae* in front of, before – more at FOR] **1 a** : (1) : earlier than : prior to : before <*Pre*cambrian> <*pre*historic> <*pre*-English> (2) : preparatory or prerequisite to <*pre*medical> <*pre*journalism> **b** : in advance : beforehand <*pre*cancel> <*pre*pay> **2 a** : in front of : anterior to <*pre*axial> <*pre*molar> **b** : front : anterior <*pre*abdomen>

re- *prefix* [ME, fr. OF, fr. L *re-*, *red-* back, again, against] **1** : again : anew <*re*tell> **2** : back : backward <*re*call>

B USING CONTEXT CLUES

Place an X in front of each correct answer. The word may be used correctly in one or both of the sentences.

1. When you add a postscript to a letter,
   ___a. you add more after the main letter.
   ___b. you add a *p.s.* to the letter.

2. To postpone a vacation is to
   ___a. put it off until later.
   ___b. forget about it.

3. A weatherman may predict a storm means
   ___a. a weatherman may know a storm is coming.
   ___b. a weatherman may know a storm has passed.

4. A mirror will reflect the sun's rays means
   ___a. the sun's rays will be turned back.
   ___b. the sun's rays will be lost.

5. An application for a bank loan must precede approval of the loan means
   ___a. you apply for the loan after you receive the money.
   ___b. you apply for the loan before you receive the money.

Check your answers with the Key on page 138.

C CHECKING THE MEANING

Read the words in the boxes. Choose the word that best completes the sentence under them. Write that word on the line. Then complete the next sentence by placing an X in front of the correct answer.

1. postpone | postscript

The man decided to ________________ his trip to Paris.
This sentence means
___a. the man will never go to Paris.
___b. the man decided to go to Italy.
___c. the man put off his trip to Paris until later.

2. predict | prevent

If drivers were more careful, they could ________________ accidents.
This sentence means
___a. careful drivers never have accidents.
___b. careful drivers can sometimes stop accidents before they happen.
___c. careful drivers often invite accidents.

3. rebuilt | recall

The old house will be ________________.
This sentence means
___a. the old house will be torn down.
___b. the old house needs no repair.
___c. the old house will look as it once did.

4. remember | reflect

The store window will ________________ the moon's light.
This sentence means
___a. the window will stop the moon's light.
___b. the window will allow the moonlight in.
___c. the window will turn the moonlight back.

5. postwar | precede

Many events ________________ a war.
This sentence means
___a. many events lead up to war.
___b. many events come during a war.
___c. many events come after a war.

Check your answers with the Key on page 138.

D COMPLETING THE SENTENCES

Choose a word from the box that best completes each sentence. Write it on the line.

predict	precede	prevent	rebuilt
reflect	recall	postpone	postscript

1. I will try to ______________________ the winner of the race.
2. The dam will ______________________ the river from flowing into town.
3. Including a ______________________ in a letter is sometimes necessary.
4. The young man asked the old woman if she wanted to __________________ him in line.
5. A rainy day may ______________________ a camping trip.

Check your answers with the Key on page 138.

E USING THE SKILL

Underline the word that best completes each sentence.

1. Heavy winds may (postpone, precede) a storm.
2. The lawyer will ask the judge to (postscript, postpone) the hearing.
3. You can (recall, prevent) tooth decay by brushing your teeth daily.
4. The light from the candle is (reflected, remembered) on the glass table.
5. The old castle is being (postponed, rebuilt) as it once was.

Check your answers with the Key on page 138.

F SUPPLEMENTARY WRITING EXERCISE

The prefixes that were taught in this lesson are:

pre-	post-	re-

Write sentences in which you use each of the prefixes in a word in the sentence.

1. ____
2. ____
3. ____

A WRITING THE WORDS

A. Write these words on the blank lines.
Then say each word.

	Write
bicycle	1. ______________
biplane	2. ______________
uniform	3. ______________
university	4. ______________
unison	5. ______________
biennial	6. ______________
monoplane	7. ______________
monologue	8. ______________
monotonous	9. ______________
United States	10. ______________

B. Each word begins with a prefix.
Write the prefix for each word.

1. ______________
2. ______________
3. ______________
4. ______________
5. ______________
6. ______________
7. ______________
8. ______________
9. ______________
10. ______________

THE PREFIXES RELATE TO **NUMBERS**.

bi- *prefix* [ME, fr. L; akin to OE *twi-*] **1 a** : two <*bi*parous> **b** : coming or occurring every two <*bi*monthly> <*bi*weekly> **c** : into two parts <*bi*sect> **2 a** : twice : doubly : on both sides <*bi*conic> <*bi*convex>> **b** : coming or occurring two times <*bi*quarterly> <*bi*weekly> – often disapproved in this sense because of the likehood of confusion with sense 1b; compare SEMI- **3** : between, involving, or affecting two (specified) symmetrical parts <*bi*aural> **4 a** : containing one (specified) constituent in double the proportion of the other constituent or in double the ordinary proportion <*bi*carbonate> **b** : DI- 2 <*bi*phenyl>

mon- *or* **mono-** \ *under stress the (1st) "o" is sometimes* ō *although not shown at individual entries* \ *comb form* [ME, fr. MF & L; MF fr. L, fr. Gk, fr. *monos* alone, single – more at MONK] **1** : one : single : alone <*mono*plane> <*mono*drama> <*mono*phobia> **2 a** : containing one (usu. specified) atom, radical, or group <*mono*hydrate> <*mono*oxide> **b** : monomolecular <*mono*film> <*mono*layer>

uni- *prefix* [ME, fr. MF, fr. L, fr. *unus* – more at ONE] : one: single <*uni*cellular>

B USING CONTEXT CLUES

Place an X in front of each correct answer. The word may be used correctly in one or both of the sentences.

1. A bicycle has
   ___a. two wheels.
   ___b. one wheel.

2. A biplane has
   ___a. one wing.
   ___b. two wings.

3. Soldiers wear the same uniform
   ___a. so they look alike.
   ___b. so they appear to be the same.

4. A university has many schools
   ___a. on one campus.
   ___b. in two buildings.

5. When we speak in unison,
   ___a. we speak separately.
   ___b. we speak together.

Check your answers with the Key on page 138.

C CHECKING THE MEANING

Read the words in the boxes. Choose the word that best completes the sentence under them. Write that word on the line. Then complete the next sentence by placing an X in front of the correct answer.

1. | bicycle | | biennial |

The flowers are ______________________.
This sentence means
___a. the flowers bloom every year.
___b. the flowers bloom every two years.
___c. the flowers bloom every three years.

2. | biplane | | unison |

The ______________________ still flew after losing one wing.
This sentence means
___a. the plane began its flight with three wings.
___b. the plane began its flight with two wings.
___c. the plane began its flight with one wing.

3. | monologue | | monotonous |

A talk-show host will often begin his show with a ______________________.
This sentence means
___a. the host will talk to another actor.
___b. the host will talk to the producer.
___c. the host will talk to his audience.

4. | uniform | | unison |

Most choir members sing in ______________________ with one another.
This sentence means
___a. each choir member sings his own song.
___b. the choir members sing as one group.
___c. choir members sing as several groups.

5. | university | | uniform |

A ______________________ may consist of several schools.
This sentence means
___a. several schools make up one school.
___b. several schools make up many schools.
___c. one school makes up several schools.

Check your answers with the Key on page 138.

D COMPLETING THE SENTENCES

Choose a word from the box that best completes each sentence. Write it on the line.

biennial	unison	uniform	monotonous
biplane	bicycle	monologue	university

1. Someone took the two wheels off Joe's ________________.
2. The comedian delivered a five-minute ________________.
3. It gets ________________ doing the same things every day.
4. The scouts in the parade marched in ________________.
5. The ________________ weeds will be gone in one year.

Check your answers with the Key on page 138.

E USING THE SKILL

Underline the word that best completes each sentence.

1. Several (monoplanes, monologues) were on the field.
2. The (uniform, United States) is a free country.
3. The (bicycle, biennial) is missing one wheel.
4. A (unison, university) is one school made up of many schools.
5. The man's (monologue, monotonous) bored the audience.

Check your answers with the Key on page 138.

F SUPPLEMENTARY WRITING EXERCISE

The prefixes that were taught in this lesson are:

uni-	mono-	bi-

Write sentences in which you use each of the prefixes in a word in the sentence.

1. ____
2. ____
3. ____

A WRITING THE WORDS

A. Write these words on the blank lines.
Then say each word.

	Write
semiskilled	1. ______________
semiannual	2. ______________
semicircle	3. ______________
multiple	4. ______________
superhuman	5. ______________
superior	6. ______________
supermarket	7. ______________
multiform	8. ______________
multitude	9. ______________
semiautomatic	10. ______________

B. Each word begins with a prefix.
Write the prefix for each word.

1. ______________
2. ______________
3. ______________
4. ______________
5. ______________
6. ______________
7. ______________
8. ______________
9. ______________
10. ______________

THESE PREFIXES ARE RELATED TO **QUANTITIES**.

multi- *comb form* [ME, fr. MF or L; MF, fr. L, fr. *multus* much, many, – more at MELIORATE] **1 a** : many : multiple : much <*multi*valent> **b** : more than two <*multi*lateral> **c** : more than one <*multi*para> **2** : many times over <*multi*millionaire>

semi- \ ˌsem-ī, ˈsem-ē,\ *prefix* [ME, fr. L; akin to OHG *sāmi-* half Gk *hēmi-*] **1 a** : precisely half of : (1) : forming a bisection of <*semi*ellipse> <*semi*oval> (2) : being a usu. vertically bisected form of (a specified architectural feature) <*semi*arch> <*semi*dome> **b** : half in quantity or value : half of or occurring halfway through (a specified period of time) <*semi*annually> <*semi*centenary> – compare BI- **2** : to some extent : partly : incompletely <*semi*civilized> <*semi*-independent> <*semi*dry> – compare DEMI-, HEMI- **3 a** : partial : incomplete : <*semi*consciousness> <*semi*darkness> **b** : having some of the characteristics of <*semi*porcelain> **c** : quasi <*semi*governmental> <*semi*monastic>

super- *prefix* [L, over, above, in addition, fr. *super* over, above, on top of – more at OVER] **1 a** : (1) : over and above : higher in quantity, quality, or degree than : more than <*super*human> (2) : in addition : extra <*super*tax> **b** (1) : exceeding or so as to exceed a norm <*super*heat> (2) : in excessive degree or intensity <*super*subtle> **c** : surpassing all or most others of its kind <*super*highway> **2 a** : situated or placed above, on, or at the top of <*super*lunary> ; *specif* : situated on the dorsal side of **b** : next above or higher <*super*tonic> **3** : having the (specified) ingredient present in a large or unusually large proportion <*super*phosphate> **4** : constituting a more inclusive category than that specified <*super*family> **5** : superior in status, title, or position <*super*power>

B USING CONTEXT CLUES

Place an X in front of each correct answer. The word may be used correctly in one or both of the sentences.

1. A semiskilled worker
   ___a. has some skills related to his work.
   ___b. is partly trained for his job.

2. A bank that pays semiannual interest
   ___a. pays interest once a year.
   ___b. pays interest twice a year.

3. If a group is asked to form a semicircle,
   ___a. the group should form a full circle.
   ___b. the group should form a half-circle.

4. If multiple copies are made for you,
   ___a. you have one copy.
   ___b. you have many copies.

5. To be considered superhuman,
   ___a. one must be weak.
   ___b. one must have great strength.

Check your answers with the Key on page 138.

C CHECKING THE MEANING

Read the words in the boxes. Choose the word that best completes the sentence under them. Write that word on the line. Then complete the next sentence by placing an X in front of the correct answer.

1. | semicircle | | supermarket |

A __________________ offers many items for purchase.
This sentence means
___a. the store is closed.
___b. the store sells one item.
___c. the store sells more than one item.

2. | multiform | | multitude |

New cars in the showroom are __________________.
This sentence means
___a. the cars have one shape.
___b. the cars have many shapes.
___c. the cars have two shapes.

3. | semiautomatic | | semicircle |

The machine is __________________.
This sentence means
___a. the machine can operate by itself.
___b. the machine needs someone to help operate it.
___c. the machine does not operate.

4. | multiform | | multitude |

A __________________ of people gathered for the party.
This sentence means
___a. a few people gathered for the party.
___b. no one gathered for the party.
___c. many gathered for the party.

5. | semicircle | | semiannual |

The team gathered in a __________________.
This sentence means
___a. the team formed a circle.
___b. the team formed a small part of a circle.
___c. the team formed half a circle.

Check your answers with the Key on page 138.

D COMPLETING THE SENTENCES

Choose a word from the box that best completes each sentence. Write it on the line.

superior	multiple	semiannual	semicircle
multiform	multitude	semiskilled	semiautomatic

1. Sue's cake won first prize in the contest because hers was ______________ to the others.
2. Criminals will often use _________________ names.
3. Some rifles are ____________________________ and fire with little help.
4. Some jobs require __________________ labor.
5. A full rainbow is in the shape of a __________________.

Check your answers with the Key on page 138.

E USING THE SKILL

Underline the word that best completes each sentence.

1. Many (semiautomatic, semiskilled) people work at home.
2. The Congress required (multiple, multitude) forms of the bill.
3. The (superior, superhuman) pie won the contest.
4. A (multiform, multitude) of people gathered for the picnic.
5. Many people receive checks (semicircle, semiannually).

Check your answers with the Key on page 138.

F SUPPLEMENTARY WRITING EXERCISE

The prefixes that were taught in this lesson are:

multi-	semi-	super-

Write sentences in which you use each of the prefixes in a word in the sentence.

1. ____
2. ____
3. ____

A WRITING THE WORDS

A. Write these words on the blank lines.
Then say each word.

Write

antidote	1. ______________
antonym	2. ______________
counterplot	3. ______________
contraband	4. ______________
antiseptic	5. ______________
antipathy	6. ______________
counteract	7. ______________
contradict	8. ______________
counterclaim	9. ______________
antibiotic	10. ______________

B Each word begins with a prefix.
Write the prefix for each word.

1. ______________
2. ______________
3. ______________
4. ______________
5. ______________
6. ______________
7. ______________
8. ______________
9. ______________
10. ______________

EACH OF THESE PREFIXES HAS A MEANING OF BEING **AGAINST** OR **OPPOSED** TO.

anti- *or* **ant-** *or* **anth-** *prefix* [*anti-* fr. ME, fr. OF & L; OF, fr. L, against, fr. Gk, fr. *anti-*; *ant-* fr. ME, fr. L, against, fr. Gk, fr. *anti-*; *anth-* fr. L, against, fr. Gk, fr. *anti* – more at ANTE] **1 a** : of the same kind but situated opposite, exerting energy in the opposite direction, or pursuing an opposite policy <*anti*clinal> **b** : one that is opposite in kind to <*anti*climax> **2 a** : opposing or hostile to in opinion, sympathy, or practice <*anti*-Semite> **b** : opposing in effect of activity <*ant*acid> <*anti*catalyst> **3** : combating or defending against <*anti*aircraft> <*anti*missile>

contra- *prefix* [ME, fr. L, fr. *contra* against, opposite – more at COUNTER] 1 : against : contrary : contrasting <*contra*diction> <*contra*distinction> **2** : pitched below normal bass <*contra*octave>

counter- *prefix* [ME *contre-*, fr. MF, fr. *contre*] **1 a** : contrary : opposite <*counter*clockwise> <*counter*march> **b** : opposing : retaliatory <*counter*irritant> <*counter*offensive> **2** : complementary : corresponding <*counter*weight> <*counter*part> **3** : duplicate : substitute <*counter*foil>

B USING CONTEXT CLUES

Place an X in front of each correct answer. The word may be used correctly in one or both of the sentences.

1. An antidote is a remedy which acts
   ___a. to spread a poison.
   ___b. against the effects of a poison.

2. An antibiotic
   ___a. produces red blood cells.
   ___b. helps fight infection.

3. To plan a counterplot is to
   ___a. plan an opposing plan.
   ___b. plan against.

4. Contraband merchandise is something
   ___a. that's against the law.
   ___b. that's illegal.

5. To use antiseptic is to use
   ___a. a substance to clean a wound.
   ___b. a substance that will spread germs.

Check your answers with the Key on page 139.

C CHECKING THE MEANING

Read the words in the boxes. Choose the word that best completes the sentence under them. Write that word on the line. Then complete the next sentence by placing an X in front of the correct answer.

1. antidote   antibiotic

The ________________ will work against the poison.
This sentence means
___a. the poison may be counteracted.
___b. the poison may spread to other parts of the body.
___c. the poison may be fatal.

2. antonym   antipathy

I was asked to find an ________________ for the word "healthy."
This sentence means
___a. I was asked to find a word that means the same as "healthy."
___b. I was asked to find a word that means the opposite of "healthy."
___c. I was asked to find a word that sounds similar to "healthy."

3. counteract   contradict

A hot bath will often ________________ the effects of a chill.
This sentence means
___a. a hot bath will never remove a chill.
___b. a hot bath will invite a chill.
___c. a hot bath will reverse the effects of a chill.

4. counterplot   contradict

I think you're wrong, therefore, I ________________ you.
This sentence means
___a. I object to your ideas.
___b. I share your ideas.
___c. I have no feelings one way or another.

5. contraband   antiseptic

Illegal merchandise is considered ________________.
This sentence means
___a. the merchandise cannot be sold legally.
___b. the merchandise is of good quality.
___c. the merchandise can be sold legally.

Check your answers with the Key on page 139.

D COMPLETING THE SENTENCES

Choose a word from the box that best completes each sentence. Write it on the line.

antidote	counteract	counterplot	contradict
antonym	contraband	antiseptic	antipathy

1. The new medicine may be an ________________ for the snake venom.
2. The word "hot" is an ________________ for the word "cold."
3. An antidote is necessary to ________________ the effects of the poison.
4. The enemy planned a ________________ to destroy us.
5. Many of the goods brought into this country are ________________.

Check your answers with the Key on page 139.

E USING THE SKILL

Underline the word that best completes each sentence.

1. An antidote is a remedy which acts to (counterplot, counteract) a poison.
2. A dictionary may give an (antipathy, antonym) for a word.
3. I do not wish to (contradict, counterclaim) you.
4. An antiseptic will (contradict, counteract) germs.
5. The old man has (contraband, antipathy) for all new ideas.

Check your answers with the Key on page 139.

F SUPPLEMENTARY WRITING EXERCISE

The prefixes that were taught in this lesson are:

anti-	contra-	counter

Write sentences in which you use each of the prefixes in a word in the sentence.

1. ____
2. ____
3. ____

A WRITING THE WORDS

A. Write these words on the blank lines.
Then say each word.

Write

compose	1. ____________
compete	2. ____________
international	3. ____________
sympathy	4. ____________
compare	5. ____________
compress	6. ____________
interstate	7. ____________
interplanetary	8. ____________
synonym	9. ____________
symphony	10. ____________

B. Each word begins with a prefix.
Write the prefix for each word.

1. ____________
2. ____________
3. ____________
4. ____________
5. ____________
6. ____________
7. ____________
8. ____________
9. ____________
10. ____________

EACH OF THESE PREFIXES SHOWS **RELATIONSHIP**.

com- *or* **col-** *or* **con-** *prefix* [ME, fr. OF, fr. L, with, together, thoroughly – more at CO-] : with : together : jointly – usu. *com-* before *b, p,* or *m* <*com*mingle>, *col-* before *l* <*col*linear>, and *con-* before other sounds <*con*centrate>

inter- *prefix* [ME *inter-, enter-,* fr. MF *inter-, entre-,* fr. L *inter-,* fr. *inter*; akin to OHG *untar* between, among, Gk *enteron* intestine, OE *in* in] **1** : between : among : in the midst <*inter*crop> <*inter*penetrate> <*inter*stellar> **2** : reciprocal <*inter*relation> : reciprocally <*inter*marry> **3** : located between <*inter*face> **4** : carried on between <*inter*national> **5** : occurring between : intervening <*inter*glacial> **6** : shared by or derived from two or more <*inter*faith> **7** : between the limits of : within <*inter*tropical>

syn- *or* **sym-** *prefix* [ME, fr. OF, fr. L, fr. Gk, fr. *syn* with, together with] **1** : with : along with : together <*syn*clinal> <*sym*petalous> **2** : at the same time <*syn*esthesia>

B USING CONTEXT CLUES

Place an X in front of each correct answer. The word may be used correctly in one or both of the sentences.

1. An <u>interstate</u>
   ___a. is a small route that is used to get from state to state.
   ___b. is a highway that is used to travel from one state to another.

2. I will <u>compose</u> a song means
   ___a. I will create a song.
   ___b. I will sing a song.

3. To <u>compete</u> in sports means
   ___a. participating in sports with others and trying to win.
   ___b. to let others succeed in the sport.

4. An <u>international</u> competition is a competition that
   ___a. competes against other cities.
   ___b. competes against other nations.

5. When you have <u>sympathy</u> for another person,
   ___a. you have different feelings than that person.
   ___b. you have the same feelings as that person.

Check your answers with the Key on page 139.

C CHECKING THE MEANING

Read the words in the boxes. Choose the word that best completes the sentence under them. Write that word on the line. Then complete the next sentence by placing an X in front of the correct answer.

1. compare | compress

The boys will __________________ the pile of papers to tie them.
This sentence means
___a. the boys will make the pile larger.
___b. the boys will make the pile smaller.
___c. the boys will make the pile even.

2. interstate | interplanetary

Space shuttles may one day become __________________________.
This sentence means
___a. space shuttles may one day move between countries.
___b. space shuttles may one day move between cities.
___c. space shuttles may one day move between planets.

3. synonym | sympathy

A __________________ for the word "switch" is "change."
This sentence means
___a. a synonym has no meaning.
___b. a synonym means the same as another word.
___c. a synonym means the opposite of another word.

4. sympathy | symphony

A __________________ orchestra is pleasant to listen to.
This sentence means
___a. the orchestra blends together well.
___b. the orchestra is very loud.
___c. the orchestra is very disappointing.

5. interstate | international

Many decisions are made at the __________________________ level.
This sentence means
___a. some decisions are made between planets.
___b. some decisions are made between nations.
___c. some decisions are made between cities.

Check your answers with the Key on page 139.

D COMPLETING THE SENTENCES

Choose a word from the box that best completes each sentence. Write it on the line.

synonym	compose	compress	international
sympathy	compete	symphony	interplanetary

1. I need a ____________________ so I can change the word but not the sentence's meaning.

2. A patient in a hospital could use a little ______________________.

3. The ______________________ flight left New York for Paris.

4. The teams will ______________________ on the football field.

5. The space shuttle left on an ______________________ flight.

Check your answers with the Key on page 139.

E USING THE SKILL

Underline the word that best completes each sentence.

1. The nurse gave the patient much (symphony, sympathy).

2. The two suits of clothes (compare, compose) in color.

3. We took (international, interstate) 10 from New York to Boston.

4. A (symphony, synonym) for "big" is "large."

5. To (compress, compete) in sports is to take part in sports.

Check your answers with the Key on page 139.

F SUPPLEMENTARY WRITING EXERCISE

The prefixes that were taught in this lesson are:

com-	inter-	sym-	syn-

Write sentences in which you use each of the prefixes in a word in the sentence.

1. ____

2. ____

3. ____

4. ____

A WRITING THE WORDS

A. Write these words on the blank lines.
Then say each word.

	Write
epidemic	1. ____________
intrastate	2. ____________
intravenous	3. ____________
intramural	4. ____________
engrave	5. ____________
epidermis	6. ____________
enclose	7. ____________
endanger	8. ____________
envelop	9. ____________
encircle	10. ____________

B. Each word begins with a prefix.
Write the prefix for each word.

1. ____________
2. ____________
3. ____________
4. ____________
5. ____________
6. ____________
7. ____________
8. ____________
9. ____________
10. ____________

THESE PREFIXES HAVE MEANINGS THAT RELATE TO **PLACE**.

en- *also* **em-** *prefix* [ME, fr. L, fr. Gk, fr. *en* in – more at IN] : in : within <*en*zootic> – usu. *em-* before *b, m,* or *p* <*em*pathy>

epi- *or* **ep-** *prefix* [ME, fr. MF & L; MF, fr. L, fr. Gk, fr. *epi* on, at, besides, after; akin to OE *eof*ot crime] **1** : upon <*epi*phyte> : besides <*epi*phenomenon> : attached to <*epi*didymis> : over <*epi*center> : outer <*epi*blast> : after <*epi*genesis> **2 a** : chemical entity related to (such) another <*epi*cholesterol> **b** : chemical entity distinguished from (such) another by having a bridge connection <*epi*chlorohydrin>

intra- \ ˌintrə , -(ˌ)tra\ *prefix* [LL, fr. L *intra*, fr. (assumed) OL *interus*, adj., inward – more at INTERIOR] **1 a** : within <*intra*continental> **b** : during <*intra*natal> **c** : between layers of <*intra*dermal> **2:** INTRO- <an *intra*muscular injection>

B USING CONTEXT CLUES

Place an X in front of each correct answer. The word may be used correctly in one or both of the sentences.

1. The flu may become an epidemic means
   ___a. the flu may strike many people.
   ___b. the flu will strike only a few people.

2. We will travel intrastate this summer means
   ___a. we will travel outside the state.
   ___b. we will travel within the state.

3. The doctor gave the patient an intravenous medicine means
   ___a. the doctor put medicine into the patient's vein.
   ___b. the doctor put medicine into the patient's mouth.

4. An intramural basketball game is played
   ___a. between students of the same school.
   ___b. between students from two different schools.

5. The jeweler will engrave the bracelet means
   ___a. the jeweler will fix the bracelet.
   ___b. the jeweler will write on the bracelet.

Check your answers with the Key on page 139.

C CHECKING THE MEANING

Read the words in the boxes. Choose the word that best completes the sentence under them. Write that word on the line. Then complete the next sentence by placing an X in front of the correct answer.

1. epidermis | epidemic

Your ________________ can become sunburned if exposed to the sun too long.
This sentence means
___a. the top of your head will become sunburned.
___b. the bottom of your feet will become sunburned.
___c. the outer layer of skin on your body will become sunburned.

2. enclose | endanger

The rancher was forced to ________________ the pasture with barbed wire.
This sentence means
___a. the rancher irrigated the grazing area.
___b. the rancher surrounded the pasture with barbed wire.
___c. the rancher removed the barbed wire from the pasture.

3. envelop | enclose

The tornado was about to ________________ the house.
This sentence means
___a. the tornado was completely surrounding the house.
___b. the tornado was about to destroy the house.
___c. the tornado would pass over the house.

4. endanger | enclose

An epidemic of measles would ________________ the lives of many people.
This sentence means
___a. an epidemic would improve people's health.
___b. an epidemic would be of little concern to the public.
___c. an epidemic would hurt or injure many people.

5. encircle | envelop

The Indians attempted to ________________ the settlers in the wagon train.
This sentence means
___a. the Indians attempted to massacre the settlers.
___b. the Indians tried to follow the wagon train.
___c. the Indians tried to surround the wagon train.

Check your answers with the Key on page 139.

D COMPLETING THE SENTENCES

Choose a word from the box that best completes each sentence. Write it on the line.

epidemic	engrave	endanger	envelop
epidermis	encircle	enclose	intramural

1. Dermatologists treat conditions of the ___________________.
2. The student body attended the ___________________ soccer game.
3. The disease was reaching ___________________ proportions.
4. Please ___________________ a check with your order.
5. I watched Greg ___________________ my initials on his desk.

Check your answers with the Key on page 139.

E USING THE SKILL

Underline the word that best completes each sentence.

1. The trucking firm was an (intramural, intrastate) operation.
2. The patient received (epidemic, intravenous) medicine.
3. The couple wanted the printer to (encircle, engrave) the invitations.
4. Riding a bicycle in the street may (envelop, endanger) your life.
5. Please (engrave, enclose) a photograph with your application form.

Check your answers with the Key on page 139.

F SUPPLEMENTARY WRITING EXERCISE

The prefixes that were taught in this lesson are:

epi-	en-	intra-

Write sentences in which you use each of the prefixes in a word in the sentence.

1. ____
2. ____
3. ____

A WRITING THE WORDS

A. Write these words on the blank lines.
Then say each word.

Write

magnified	1. ____________
telegraph	2. ____________
telepathy	3. ____________
magnificent	4. ____________
microscope	5. ____________
microbe	6. ____________
microwave	7. ____________
microphone	8. ____________
telephone	9. ____________
television	10. ____________

B. Each word begins with a prefix.
Write the prefix for each word.

1. ____________
2. ____________
3. ____________
4. ____________
5. ____________
6. ____________
7. ____________
8. ____________
9. ____________
10. ____________

THESE PREFIXES ARE RELATED TO **SIZE** AND **DISTANCE**.

mag·ni·fi·ca·tion \ ˌmag-nə - fə - ˈkā -shən \ *n* **1** : the act of magnifying **2 a** : the state of being magnified **b** : the apparent enlargement of an object by an optical instrument

micr- *or* **micro-** *comb form* [ME *micro-*, fr. L, fr. Gk *mikr-, mikro,* fr. *mikros, smikros* small, short; akin to OE *smēalic* careful, exquisite] **1 a** : small : minute <*micro*film> **b** : used for or involving minute quantities or variations <*micro*barograph> **c** : minutely <*micro*level> **2** : one millionth part of a (specified) unit <*micro*gram> <*micro*ohm> **3 a** : using microscopy <*micro*dissection> : used in microscopy **b** : revealed by or having its structure discernible only by microscopical examination <*micro*organism> **4** : abnormally small <*micro*cyte> **5** : of or relating to a small area <*micro*climate> **6** : employed in or connected with microphotography or microfilming <*micro*copy>

tele- *or* **tel-** *comb form* [NL, fr. Gk *tēle-, tēl-*, fr. *tēle* far off – more at PALE] **1** : distant : at a distance : over a distance <*tele*gram> <*tele*sthesia> **2 a** : telegraph <*tele*typewriter> **b** : television <*tele*cast> **c** : telecommunication <*tele*man>

B USING CONTEXT CLUES

Place an X in front of each correct answer. The word may be used correctly in one or both of the sentences.

1. When something is magnified,
   ___a. it becomes larger.
   ___b. it becomes clearer.

2. The telegraph
   ___a. is used to send messages from room to room.
   ___b. is used to send messages over long distances.

3. Telepathy is
   ___a. a means of sending messages over long distances without writing.
   ___b. a means of sending messages over long distances with the mind.

4. The wedding was magnificent means
   ___a. the wedding was a small affair limited to family members.
   ___b. the wedding was a large affair.

5. A microscope
   ___a. makes small images larger.
   ___b. makes large images smaller.

Check your answers with the Key on page 140.

C CHECKING THE MEANING

Read the words in the boxes. Choose the word that best completes the sentence under them. Write that word on the line. Then complete the next sentence by placing an X in front of the correct answer.

1. microscope   microbe

A ________________ cannot be seen by the naked eye.
This sentence means
___a. you must wear glasses to see it.
___b. you will become blind if you look at it with the naked eye.
___c. it is too small to be seen with the naked eye.

2. microwave   microphone

A ________________ condenses sound and makes it louder.
This sentence means
___a. a document condenses sound and makes it louder.
___b. a vibration condenses sound and makes it louder.
___c. an instrument condenses sound and makes it louder.

3. telegraph   telephone

When listening on the ________________, distance is no problem.
This sentence means
___a. listening at a distance is a problem.
___b. talking at a distance is a problem.
___c. listening at a distance is no problem.

4. television   telepathy

To watch ________________ is enjoyable.
This sentence means
___a. watching pictures is enjoyable.
___b. playing a game is enjoyable.
___c. listening from far away is enjoyable.

5. Microphones   Microwaves

________________ can be used to generate heat.
This sentence means
___a. microwaves can be used to keep food from spoiling.
___b. microphones can cook a meal in half the time of a conventional oven.
___c. microwaves can be used to produce heat.

Check your answers with the Key on page 140.

D COMPLETING THE SENTENCES

Choose a word from the box that best completes each sentence. Write it on the line.

telegraph	microscope	magnified	television
telepathy	microbe	telephone	magnificent

1. A scientist uses a microscope to try and identify a ________________.
2. In order to see a microbe, it must be ________________.
3. The school dance was planned so that it would be a ________________ affair.
4. A ________________ enlarges things not visible to the naked eye.
5. The ________________ makes it possible for us to hear friends far away.

Check your answers with the Key on page 140.

E USING THE SKILL

Underline the word that best completes each sentence.

1. Emily wanted a (microbe, microwave) oven for Christmas.
2. Morse code is used when a message is sent by (television, telegraph).
3. The psychic sent messages using mental (telephone, telepathy).
4. When people watch (telephone, television) they use their eyes and ears.
5. The (microscope, microphone) made the singer's voice louder.

Check your answers with the Key on page 140.

F SUPPLEMENTARY WRITING EXERCISE

The prefixes that were taught in this lesson are:

tele-	micro-	magni-

Write the sentences in which you use each of the prefixes in a word in the sentence.

1. ____
2. ____
3. ____

A WRITING THE WORDS

A. Write these words on the blank lines. Then say each word.

Write

	Write
inject	1. ______
detract	2. ______
remit	3. ______
admit	4. ______
reject	5. ______
submit	6. ______
subtract	7. ______
retract	8. ______
permit	9. ______
commit	10. ______

B. Each word contains a word root or word stem. Write the word root or the word stem for each word.

1. ______
2. ______
3. ______
4. ______
5. ______
6. ______
7. ______
8. ______
9. ______
10. ______

THESE ROOTS OR STEMS HAVE MEANINGS THAT RELATE TO AN **ACTION**.

re-ject \ ri-ˊjekt \ *vt* [ME *rejecten*, fr. L *rejectus*, pp. of *reicere*, fr. *re-* + *jacere* to throw – more at JET] **1 a** : to refuse to accept, consider, submit to, take for some purpose, or use <thought about her suggestion and then ~*ed* it> <~ a manuscript> <~ *ed* the weevily grain as unfit for use> **b** : to refuse to hear, receive, or admit : REBUFF, REPELL <parents who ~ their children> **c** : to refuse lover or spouse **2** *obs* : to cast off **3** : to throw back : REPULSE **4** : to spew out **syn** see DECLINE **ant** accept : choose

sub-mit \ səb-ˊmit \ *vb* **sub-mit-ted; sub-mit-ting** [ME *submitten*, fr. L *submittere* to lower, submit, fr. *sub* + *mittere* to send – more at SMITE] *vt* **1 a** : to yield to governance or authority **b** : to subject to a regime, condition, or practice <the metal was *submitted* for analysis> **2 a** : to commit to another (as for decision or judgment) <~ a question to the court> **b** : to make available : OFFER <~ a bid on a contract> < ~ a report> **c** : to put forward as an opinion : AFFIRM <we ~ that the charge is not proved>~*vi* **1 a** : to yield oneself to the authority of or will of another **b** : to permit oneself to be subjected to something

sub-tract \ səb-ˊtrakt \ *vb* [L *subtractus*, pp. of *subtrahere* to draw from beneath, withdraw, fr. *sub* + *trahere* to draw – more at DRAW] *vt* : to take away by deducting <~5 from 9>~*vi* : to perform a subtraction – **sub-tract-er** *n*

B USING CONTEXT CLUES

Place an X in front of each correct answer. The word may be used correctly in one or both of the sentences.

1. The doctor will inject the antidote into the man's arm means
   ___a. the antidote must be thrust into the man's arm.
   ___b. the antidote must be taken from the man's arm.

2. A black eye will detract from your looks means
   ___a. a black eye will add to your looks.
   ___b. a black eye will take away from your looks.

3. You must remit money for the TV offer means
   ___a. you must send money.
   ___b. you must ask for money.

4. This ticket will admit you to the concert means
   ___a. the ticket will let you pass through to the concert.
   ___b. the ticket will not let you pass through to the concert.

5. An inspector will reject poor quality means
   ___a. an inspector will refuse to accept poorly made items.
   ___b. an inspector will inspect poorly made items.

Check your answers with the Key on page 140.

C CHECKING THE MEANING

Read the words in the boxes. Choose the word that best completes the sentence under them. Write that word on the line. Then complete the next sentence by placing an X in front of the correct answer.

1. submit   remit

Please __________________ your entry for the contest.
This sentence means
___a. send in your entry for the contest.
___b. send back your name for the contest.
___c. send money with your entry.

2. subtract   retract

The lawyer will __________________ his statement to the newspaper.
This sentence means
___a. the lawyer will add to his statement.
___b. the lawyer will take back his statement.
___c. the lawyer will never make another statement.

3. permit   commit

To park your car, you must have a __________________.
This sentence means
___a. you must have time to park.
___b. you must have something that allows you to park.
___c. you must have money to park.

4. commit   subtract

The boss will not allow you to __________________ yourself to another job.
This sentence means
___a. the boss will not allow you to spend time on a different job.
___b. the boss will allow you to spend time on another job.
___c. the boss will not allow you to work at all.

5. reject   inject

The judge will __________________ your innocent plea.
This sentence means
___a. the judge will listen to you.
___b. the judge will accept your plea.
___c. the judge will throw out your plea.

Check your answers with the Key on page 140.

D COMPLETING THE SENTENCES

Choose a word from the box that best completes each sentence. Write it on the line.

inject	detract	remit	permit
reject	subtract	admit	commit

1. This ticket will __________________ you to the concert.

2. The inspector will __________________ the car with the poor paint job.

3. Will you __________________ yourself to the cause of freedom?

4. Please __________________ one dollar with your application form.

5. If you __________________ 10 from your total, you will arrive at the correct number.

Check your answers with the Key on page 140.

E USING THE SKILL

Underline the word that best completes each sentence.

1. Will you (permit, commit) me to go to the game?

2. The doctor will (reject, inject) the medicine into the man's arm.

3. You must (admit, submit) your entry fee by March 31st.

4. Old paint will (retract, detract) from the home's beauty.

5. The man will (subtract, retract) the statement he gave to the police.

Check your answers with the Key on page 140.

F SUPPLEMENTARY WRITING EXERCISE

The roots that were taught in this lesson are:

-ject	-tract	-mit

Write sentences in which you use each of the roots in a word in the sentence.

1. ____

2. ____

3. ____

A WRITING THE WORDS

A. Write these words on the blank lines.
Then say each word.

Write

factory	1. ______________
factual	2. ______________
suspend	3. ______________
conclude	4. ______________
appendix	5. ______________
manufacture	6. ______________
expend	7. ______________
exclude	8. ______________
depend	9. ______________
include	10. ______________

B. Each word contains a word root or word stem.
Write the word root or the word stem for each word.

1. ______________

2. ______________

3. ______________

4. ______________

5. ______________

6. ______________

7. ______________

8. ______________

9. ______________

10. ______________

THESE ROOTS OR STEMS HAVE MEANINGS THAT RELATE TO AN **ACTION**.

ex-clude \ iks-ˈklüd \ *vt* **ex-clud-ed; ex-clud-ing** [ME *excluden*, fr. L *excludere*, fr. *ex-* + *claudere* to close – more at CLOSE] **1 a** : to shut out **b** : to bar from participation, consideration, or inclusion **2** : to expel esp. from a place of position previously occupied –**ex-clud-er** *n*

ex-pend \ ik-ˈspend \ *vt* [ME *expenden*, fr. L *expendere* to weigh out, expend, fr. *ex-* + *pendere* to weigh – more at SPAN] **1** : to pay out : SPEND <the social services upon which public revenue is ~ *ed* – J.A. Hobson> **2** : to consume by use : use up <projects on which he ~ *ed* great energy> – **ex-pend-er** *n*

fact \ ˈfakt \ *n* [L *factum*, fr. neut. of *factus*, pp. of *facere*] **1** : a thing done ; as **a** : CRIME <accessory after the ~ > **b** : *obs* : FEAT **c** : *archaic* : ACTION **2** *archaic* : PERFORMANCE, DOING **3** : the quality of being actual : ACTUALITY <a question of ~ brings on actual evidence> **4 a** : something that has actual existence <space travel is now a~> **b** : an actual occurrence : EVENT <the ~ of his presence is proven by witnesses> **5** : a piece of information presented as having objective reality – **fac-tic-i-ty** \ fak-ˈtis-ət-ē \ *n* – **in fact** : in truth : ACTUALLY

B USING CONTEXT CLUES

Place an X in front of each correct answer. The word may be used correctly in one or both of the sentences.

1. A <u>factory</u> is a place
   ___a. where things are made
   ___b. where furniture is made.

2. I must write a <u>factual</u> report means
   ___a. my report must be true.
   ___b. my report must be done quickly.

3. He will <u>suspend</u> himself from the monkey bars means
   ___a. he will climb on the monkey bars.
   ___b. he will hang from the monkey bars.

4. The class meeting will <u>conclude</u> means
   ___a. the class meeting will continue.
   ___b. the class meeting will end.

5. The <u>appendix</u> of a book is
   ___a. something added to the end of a book.
   ___b. something taken away from the end of the book.

Check your answers with the Key on page 140.

C CHECKING THE MEANING

Read the words in the boxes. Choose the word that best completes the sentence under them. Write that word on the line. Then complete the next sentence by placing an X in front of the correct answer.

1. expend depend

The boy could always __________________ on his father.
This sentence means
___a. the boy did not get along with his father.
___b. the boy could rely on his father.
___c. the boy did not agree with his father about anything.

2. suspend expend

Edward will __________________ much energy jogging.
This sentence means
___a. Edward will use up much energy jogging.
___b. Edward will use little energy jogging.
___c. Edward will go jogging to restore his energy.

3. conclude exclude

We will __________________ children from the party.
This sentence means
___a. there will be no children at the party.
___b. we will invite all the children to the party.
___c. some children will attend the party.

4. depend expend

You must __________________ on yourself to answer the questions correctly.
This sentence means
___a. you must rely on yourself to answer the questions correctly.
___b. you must trust your friend for the answers.
___c. the teacher will assist you with the questions.

5. include exclude

I will __________________ tomatoes in the salad.
This sentence means
___a. I will put tomatoes in the salad.
___b. I will not put tomatoes in the salad.
___c. I will make a tomato salad.

Check your answers with the Key on page 140.

D COMPLETING THE SENTENCES

Choose a word from the box that best completes each sentence. Write it on the line.

suspend	appendix	include	manufacture
factual	expend	depend	conclude

1. The __________________ of cars is an important industry.
2. The man gave a __________________ report to the officer.
3. A book provides extra information in its __________________.
4. Many meetings __________________ with coffee and dessert.
5. You must __________________ on yourself to make good decisions.

Check your answers with the Key on page 140.

E USING THE SKILL

Underline the word that best completes each sentence.

1. I will (expend, depend) much energy running the race.
2. A (factual, factory) will produce the bicycle.
3. I will (expend, suspend) the light directly over the table's center.
4. We will (include, conclude) the dance with one last number.
5. To (include, exclude) a person is to leave that person out.

Check your answers with the Key on page 140.

F SUPPLEMENTARY WRITING EXERCISE

The roots that were taught in this lesson are:

-fact	-clude	-pend

Write sentences in which you use each of the roots in a word in the sentence.

1. ____
2. ____
3. ____

A WRITING THE WORDS

A. Write these words on the blank lines.
Then say each word.

	Write
deposit	1. ______________
revolve	2. ______________
involve	3. ______________
position	4. ______________
resolve	5. ______________
proposition	6. ______________
evolve	7. ______________
solvent	8. ______________
disposition	9. ______________
dissolve	10. ______________

B. Each word contains a word root or word stem. Write the word root or the word stem for each word.

1. ______________
2. ______________
3. ______________
4. ______________
5. ______________
6. ______________
7. ______________
8. ______________
9. ______________
10. ______________

THESE ROOTS OR STEMS HAVE MEANINGS THAT RELATE TO AN **ACTION**.

po-si-tion \ pə-ˈzish-ən \ *n* [MF, fr. L *position-, posito,* fr. *postus*, pp. of *ponere* to lay down, put, place, fr. (assumed) OL *posinere*, fr. *po-* away (akin to Gk *apo-*) + L *sinere* to lay, leave – more at SITE] **1** : an act of placing or arranging : as **a** : the laying down of a proposition or thesis **b** : an arranging in order **2** : a point of view adopted and held to <made his ~ on the issue clear> **3 a** : the point or area occupied by a physical object <took her ~ at the head of the line> **b** : a certain arrangement of bodily parts <rose to a standing ~ > **4 a** : relative place, situation, or standing <is now in a ~ to make important decisions on his own> **b** : social or official rank or status **c** : EMPLOYMENT, JOB **d** : a situation that confers advantage or preference

re-solve \ ri-ˈzälv, -ˈzȯlv \ *vb* **re-solved; re-solv-ing** [L *resolvere* to unloose, dissolve, fr. *re-* + *solvere* to loosen, release – more at SOLVE] *vt* **1** : *obs* : DISSOLVE, MELT **2 a** : to break up : SEPARATE <the prism *resolved* the light into a play of color> *also* : to change by disintegration **b** : to reduce by analysis < ~ the problem into sample elements> **3** : to cause resolution of (as inflammation) **4 a** : to deal with successfully : clear up < ~ doubts> < ~ a dispute> **b** : to find an answer to **c** : to make clear or understandable **d** : to find a mathematical solution to **e** : to split up (as a vector) into two or more components esp. in assigned directions **5** : to reach a firm decision about <~ to get more sleep> **6 a** : to declare or decide by a formal resolution and vote **b** : to change by resolution or formal vote **7** : to make (as voice parts) progress from dissonance to consonance **8** : to work out the resolution of (as a play)

re-volve \ri-ˈvälv, -ˈvȯlv \ *vb* **re-volved; re-volv-ing** [ME *revolven*, fr. L *revolvere* to roll back, cause to return, fr. *re-* + *volvere* to roll – more at VOLUBLE] *vt* **1** : to turn over at length in the mind : PONDER < ~ a scheme> **2 a** : to cause to go round in an orbit **b** : to cause to turn around on or as if on an axis : ROTATE *vi* **1** : RECUR **2 a** : to ponder something **b** : to remain under condsideration <ideas *revolved* in his mind> **3 a** : to move in a curved path around a center or axis **b** : to turn or roll around on an axis **4** : to center on : have as a main point <the dispute *revolved* around wages> – **re-volv-able** \ -ˈväl-və-bəl, -ˈvol-\ adj

B USING CONTEXT CLUES

Place an X in front of each correct answer. The word may be used correctly in one or both of the sentences.

1. When you deposit money in the bank,
   ___a. you take money from the bank.
   ___b. you put money in the bank.

2. The merry-go-round revolves means
   ___a. the merry-go-round goes up and down.
   ___b. the merry-go-round turns 'round and 'round.

3. When you involve yourself in a sport, it means
   ___a. you turn away from the sport.
   ___b. you turn toward the sport.

4. The captain found his position on the map means
   ___a. the captain found his airplane on the map.
   ___b. the captain found his place on the map.

5. When you resolve a fight,
   ___a. you are free to turn away from the fight.
   ___b. you are committed to fight again.

Check your answers with the Key on page 141.

C CHECKING THE MEANING

Read the words in the boxes. Choose the word that best completes the sentence under them. Write that word on the line. Then complete the next sentence by placing an X in front of the correct answer.

1. deposit | position

Your __________________ on the map is in North America.
This sentence means
___a. you are leaving North America.
___b. you are in North America.
___c. you have left North America.

2. proposition | solution

Ralph made his partner a ____________________.
This sentence means
___a. Ralph made his partner lunch.
___b. Ralph proposed to his partner.
___c. Ralph gave his partner something to consider.

3. evolve | resolve

A good plan will ____________________ as you think about the problem.
This sentence means
___a. a good plan will not be possible.
___b. a good plan will turn up.
___c. a good plan will always be there.

4. solvent | solution

Dishwasher soap is a ____________________ and will clean the dirty pan.
This sentence means
___a. dishwasher soap is a lubricant.
___b. dishwasher soap will loosen food from the pan.
___c. dishwasher soap will disinfect the pan.

5. solution | dissolve

A ____________________ of soap and water will clean dishes.
This sentence means
___a. soap will clean dishes.
___b. water will clean dishes.
___c. soap and water combined will clean dishes.

Check your answers with the Key on page 141.

D COMPLETING THE SENTENCES

Choose a word from the box that best completes each sentence. Write it on the line.

deposit	position	revolve	dissolve
proposition	resolve	evolve	disposition

1. The man made a ________________ to buy out his partner.
2. To ________________ a problem is to find a remedy for the problem.
3. The Earth will continue to ________________ around the sun.
4. Pete's nasty ________________ cost him many friendships.
5. Dad took his ________________ at the head of the table.

Check your answers with the Key on page 141.

E USING THE SKILL

Underline the word that best completes each sentence.

1. The woman made a (position, deposit) at the bank.
2. I will continue to (involve, revolve) myself in sports.
3. A plan will (revolve, evolve) as you work to solve a problem.
4. The mayor's (deposit, proposition) found favor with the people of the city.
5. Sugar will (revolve, dissolve) in water when stirred.

Check your answers with the Key on page 141.

F SUPPLEMENTARY WRITING EXERCISE

The roots that were taught in this lesson are:

-posit	-volve	-solve

Write sentences in which you use each of the roots in a word in the sentence.

1. ____
2. ____
3. ____

A WRITING THE WORDS

A. Write these words on the blank lines. Then say each word.

Write

retain	1. ______
demote	2. ______
prelude	3. ______
interlude	4. ______
contain	5. ______
obtain	6. ______
emotion	7. ______
postlude	8. ______
delude	9. ______
exclude	10. ______

B. Each word contains a word root or a word stem. Write the word root or the word stem for each word.

1. ______
2. ______
3. ______
4. ______
5. ______
6. ______
7. ______
8. ______
9. ______
10. ______

THESE ROOTS OR STEMS HAVE MEANINGS THAT RELATE TO AN **ACTION**.

con-tain \ kən-ˈtān \ *vb* [ME, *conteinen*, fr. OF *contenir*, fr. L *continēre* to hold together, hold in, contain, fr. *com-* + *tenere* to hold – more at THIN] *vt* **1** : to keep within limits : hold back or hold down : as **a** : RESTRAIN, CONTROL **b** : CHECK, HALT **c** to follow successfully a policy of containment toward **d** : to prevent (as an enemy or opponent) from advancing or from making a successful attack **2 a** : to have within : HOLD **b** : COMPRISE, INCLUDE **3 a** : to be divisible by usu. without a remainder **b** : ENCLOSE, BOUND ~ *vi* : to restrain oneself – **con-tain-able** \ -ˈtā-ne-bel \ *adj*

emo-tion \ i-ˈmō-shən \ *n* [MF, fr. *emouvoir* to stir up, fr. L *exmovēre* to move away, disturb, fr. *ex-* + *movēre* to move] **1 a** : *obs* : DISTURBANCE **b** : EXCITEMENT **2 a** : the affective aspects of consciousness : FEELING **b** : a state of feeling **c** : a psychic and physical reaction (as anger or fear) subjectively experienced as strong feeling and physiologically involving changes that prepare the body for immediate vigorous action **syn** see FEELING

in-ter-lude \ ˈint-ər-ˌlüd \ *n* [ME, *enterlude*, fr. ML *interludum*, fr. L *inter-* + *ludus* play – more at LUDICROUS] **1 a** : an entertainment of a light or farcical character introduced between the acts of an old mystery or morality play or forming a feature of a festival or fete **b** : a farce or comedy derived from these entertainments **2** : a performance or entertainment between the acts of a play **3** : an intervening or interruptive period, space, or event : INTERVAL **4** : a musical composition inserted between the parts of a longer composition, a drama, or a religious service

B USING CONTEXT CLUES

Place an X in front of each correct answer. The word may be used correctly in one or both of the sentences.

1. The dam will <u>retain</u> the water means
   ___a. the dam will let the water through.
   ___b. the dam will hold the water back.

2. The captain will <u>demote</u> the sergeant means
   ___a. the sergeant will move up in rank.
   ___b. the sergeant will move down in rank.

3. The thunder was a <u>prelude</u> to the storm means
   ___a. the thunder sounded before the storm hit.
   ___b. the thunder sounded after the storm hit.

4. The play had a musical <u>interlude</u> means
   ___a. music was played after the play ended.
   ___b. music was played between the acts of the play.

5. The box <u>contained</u> the toys means
   ___a. the box did not hold all the toys.
   ___b. the box held all the toys.

Check your answers with the Key on page 141.

C CHECKING THE MEANING

Read the words in the boxes. Choose the word that best completes the sentence under them. Write that word on the line. Then complete the next sentence by placing an X in front of the correct answer.

1. | retain | | obtain |

I wish to __________________ a new bicycle.
This sentence means
___a. I wish to sell a new bicycle.
___b. I wish to get a new bicycle.
___c. I wish to give away a new bicycle.

2. | demote | | emotion |

The actor used __________________ to convey rage to the audience.
This sentence means
___a. the actor used a script to convey rage.
___b. the actor used a prompter to convey rage.
___c. the actor used his feelings to convey rage.

3. | delude | | prelude |

A marriage proposal is a __________________ to marriage.
This sentence means
___a. the proposal comes after the marriage.
___b. the proposal comes before the marriage.
___c. the proposal comes during the marriage.

4. | delude | | interlude |

The teacher will not __________________ you about your test score.
This sentence means
___a. the teacher will not discuss your test score with you.
___b. the teacher will tell you the truth about your test score.
___c. the teacher will not examine your test.

5. | exclude | | obtain |

The coach intends to __________________ me from tonight's game.
This sentence means
___a. I will be playing in tonight's game.
___b. I will not be playing in tonight's game.
___c. I will be playing in tomorrow's game.

Check your answers with the Key on page 141.

D COMPLETING THE SENTENCES

Choose a word from the box that best completes each sentence. Write it on the line.

retain	demote	prelude	delude
obtain	emotion	postlude	exclude

1. The tool rental center will ________________ your deposit until you return the tools.
2. The pianist will play a ________________ after the play.
3. An actor imparts much ________________ in his work.
4. The girls didn't mean to ________________ me from the group.
5. The boss may ________________ you if you don't do the job right.

Check your answers with the Key on page 141.

E USING THE SKILL

Underline the word that best completes each sentence.

1. Women make every effort to (obtain, retain) their youthful look.
2. A (interlude, prelude) is an introdution to something.
3. We will have a musical (postlude, interlude) after Act III of the play.
4. Don't let him (delude, exclude) you into believing his story.
5. Marty will (delude, obtain) a license when he turns 18.

Check your answers with the Key on page 141.

F SUPPLEMENTARY WRITING EXERCISE.

The roots that were taught in this lesson are:

-tain	-mote	-lude

Write sentences in which you use each of the roots in a word in the sentence.

1. ____
2. ____
3. ____

A WRITING THE WORDS

A. Write these words on the blank lines.
Then say each word.

	Write
progress	1. ____________
proceed	2. ____________
intercede	3. ____________
conduct	4. ____________
recede	5. ____________
regress	6. ____________
digress	7. ____________
produce	8. ____________
induct	9. ____________
exceed	10. ____________

B. Each word contains a word root or word stem.
Write the word root or the word stem for each word.

1. ____________
2. ____________
3. ____________
4. ____________
5. ____________
6. ____________
7. ____________
8. ____________
9. ____________
10. ____________

THESE ROOTS OR STEMS HAVE MEANINGS THAT RELATE TO AN **ACTION**.

con-duct \ kən ˈdəkt \ *vb* [alter, (influenced by L *conductus*) of earlier *conduit, condit*, fr. ME *conduiten, conditen*, fr. *conduit, condit*, – more at CONDUCT] *vt* **1** : to bring by or as if by leading : LEAD, GUIDE, ESCORT <I made a bridge to a rock whence I can reach the other side, so I shall ~ the lambs that way – Rachel Henning> **2 a** : to lead as a commander <~ a siege> **b** : to have the direction of : RUN, MANAGE, DIRECT <~ a scientific experiment> ***syn*** see in addition BEHAVE

pro-ceed \ prō-ˈsēd, prə- \ *vt* [ME *proceden*, fr. MF *proceder*, fr. L *procedre*, fr. *pro-* forward + *cedere* to go – more at PRO-, CEDE] **1** : to come forth from a source : ISSUE **2 a** : to continue after a pause or interruption **b** : to go on in an orderly regulated way **3 a** : to begin and carry on an action, process, or movement **b** : to be in the process of being accomplished **4** : to move along a course : ADVANCE ***syn*** see SPRING

pro-duce \prə-ˈd(y)üs prō- \ *vb* **pro-duced; pro-duc-ing** [ME (Sc) *producen*, fr. L *producere*, fr. *pro-* forward + *ducere* to lead – more at TOW] *vt* **1** : to offer to view or notice : EXHIBIT **2** : to give birth or rise to : YIELD **3** : to extend in length, area, or volume <~ a side of a triangle> **4** : to present to the public on the stage or screen or over radio or television **5** : to give being, form, or shape to : MAKE : *esp* : MANUFACTURE **6** : to accrue or cause to accrue ~ *vi* : to bear, make or yield something – more at PRODUCT

[1]**pro-gress** \ prə-ˈgres \ *vi* **1** : to move forward : PROCEED **2** : to develop to a higher, better, or more advanced degree
[2]**pro-gress** \ ˈprä-grės\ to go forth; go forward; advance

B USING CONTEXT CLUES

Place an X in front of each correct answer. The word may be used correctly in one or both of the sentences.

1. To make progress
   ___a. is to move forward.
   ___b. is to move backward.

2. When you proceed along a path,
   ___a. you move backward.
   ___b. you move forward.

3. When you intercede in a fight between two people,
   ___a. you move away from the fight.
   ___b. you move between the fighters.

4. When a person conducts a meeting,
   ___a. he leads each person in the meeting.
   ___b. he leads all the people together.

5. The water level will recede means
   ___a. the water level will rise.
   ___b. the water level will go down.

Check your answers with the Key on page 141.

C CHECKING THE MEANING

Read the words in the boxes. Choose the word that best completes the sentence under them. Write that word on the line. Then complete the next sentence by placing an X in front of the correct answer.

1. progress | regress

The student made ________________ in school this year.
This sentence means
___a. the student did worse this year.
___b. the student improved this year.
___c. the student failed this year.

2. digress | intercede

A poor speaker will often ________________ many times from the main subject.
This sentence means
___a. a poor speaker will stick to the main subject.
___b. a poor speaker abandons the main subject.
___c. a poor speaker strays from the main subject.

3. produce | induct

The farmer hopes to ________________ many crops this year.
This sentence means
___a. the farmer hopes to bring forth many crops.
___b. the farmer hopes to destroy his crops.
___c. the farmer hopes to transport his crops this year.

4. recede | intercede

The water level will ________________ as the rain stops.
This sentence means
___a. the water level will rise.
___b. the water level will remain the same.
___c. the water level will go down.

5. exceed | proceed

A good driver will not ________________ the speed limit.
This sentence means
___a. a good driver pays no attention to his speed.
___b. a good driver will not go over the speed limit.
___c. a good driver will drive well under the speed limit.

Check your answers with the Key on page 141.

D COMPLETING THE SENTENCES

Choose a word from the box that best completes each sentence. Write it on the line.

progress	exceed	intercede	conduct
regress	recede	induct	produce

1. This year's cotton crop will ________________ last year's poor crop.
2. Parents often ________________ in their children's quarrels.
3. The scoutmaster will ________________ the Cub Scout into the Boy Scouts.
4. You must not ________________ in your studies if you expect to do well.
5. Dan is making steady ________________ on the antique car he's restoring.

Check your answers with the Key on page 141.

E USING THE SKILL

Underline the word that best completes each sentence.

1. A poor writer will often (progress, digress) from the main topic.
2. A driver should not (recede, exceed) the speed limit.
3. The president will (conduct, induct) the new members into the club.
4. The magician will (produce, regress) a rabbit from his hat.
5. If you don't review your work, you will (progress, regress) in your schoolwork.

Check your answers with the Key on page 141.

F SUPPLEMENTARY WRITING EXERCISE

The roots that were taught in this lesson are:

-gress	-cede	-duct	-duce

Write sentences in which you use each of the roots in a word in the sentence.

1. ____
2. ____
3. ____
4. ____

A WRITING THE WORDS

Write these words on the blank lines.
Then say each word.

Write

transport	1. ______________
import	2. ______________
repel	3. ______________
propel	4. ______________
confuse	5. ______________
refund	6. ______________
refuse	7. ______________
report	8. ______________
impel	9. ______________
deport	10. ______________

B. Each word contains a word root or word stem. Write the word root or the word stem for each word.

1. ______________
2. ______________
3. ______________
4. ______________
5. ______________
6. ______________
7. ______________
8. ______________
9. ______________
10. ______________

THESE ROOTS OR STEMS HAVE MEANINGS THAT RELATE TO AN **ACTION**.

pro-pel \ prə-ˈpel \ *vt* **pro-pelled; pro-pel-ling** [ME *propellen*, fr. L *propellere*, fr. *pro-* before + *pellere* to drive – more at FELT] **1** : to drive forward or onward by means of a force that imparts motion **2** : to urge on : MOTIVATE ***syn*** see PUSH

re-fuse \ ri-ˈfyüz \ *vb* **re-fused; re-fus-ing** [ME *refusen*, fr. MF *refuser*, fr. (assumed) VL *refusare*, fr. L *refusus*, pp. of *refundere* to pour back] *vt* **1** : to express oneself as unwilling to accept <~ a gift> <~ a promotion> **2 a** : to show or express unwillingness to do or comply with <the motor *refused* to start> **b** : DENY <they were *refused* admittance to the game> **3** *obs* : to give up : RENOUNCE **4** : *of a horse* : to decline to jump or leap over~*vi* : to withhold acceptance, compliance, or permission ***syn*** see **DECLINE** – **re-fus-er** *n*

re-fund \ ˈrē fənd *sometimes* rə̇f- *or* rēˈf- \ *n* *-s* **1** : the act of refunding (giving back) **2** : a sum that is paid back : REPAYMENT

trans-port \ tran(t)s- ˈpō(ə)rt, tran(t)s- \ *vt* [ME *transporten*, fr. MF or L; MF *transporter*, fr. L *transportare*, fr. *trans* + *portare* to carry - more at FARE] **1** : to transfer or convey from one place to another <mechanisms of ~ ing ions across a living membrane> **2** : to carry away with strong and often intensely pleasant emotion **3** : to send to a penal colony overseas – **trans-port-abil-i-ty** \ (ˈ)tran(t)s-ˌpōrt-ə-ˈbil-ət ē, -ˌpȯrt- \ *n* – **trans-port-able** \ tran(t)s-ˈpōrt-ə-bəl, - ˈpȯrt- \ *adj* ***syn*** see CARRY

B USING CONTEXT CLUES

Place an X in front of each correct answer. The word may be used correctly in one or both of the sentences.

1. The train will transport the cars means
   ___a. the train will carry the cars from one place to another.
   ___b. the train will destroy the cars.

2. The United States will import many foreign goods means
   ___a. the United States will bring foreign goods into the country.
   ___b. the United States will send many goods to foreign countries.

3. The spear gun was used to repel the shark means
   ___a. the spear gun drove the shark closer.
   ___b. the spear gun drove the shark back.

4. The motor will propel the car means
   ___a. the motor will move the car backward.
   ___b. the motor will move the car forward.

5. When you confuse a person,
   ___a. you make that person understand.
   ___b. you give that person a mixed-up feeling.

Check your answers with the Key on page 142.

C CHECKING THE MEANING

Read the words in the boxes. Choose the word that best completes the sentence under them. Write that word on the line. Then complete the next sentence by placing an X in front of the correct answer.

1. refund refuse

The boy has a __________________ coming for the return of the soda bottles.
This sentence means
___a. the boy has more bottles to collect.
___b. the boy has money coming back.
___c. the boy has no money coming back.

2. report import

When we get the __________________, we will act on the business.
This sentence means
___a. when the test is returned, we will act.
___b. when we receive the papers, we will act.
___c. when we get the manual, we will act.

3. repel impel

Something inside a man will __________________ that man to do what is right.
This sentence means
___a. something inside a man tells him what to do.
___b. something inside a man forces him want to do the right thing.
___c. something inside a man drives him to do what is right.

4. confuse refuse

A good student will never __________________ extra help.
This sentence means
___a. a good student always welcomes extra help.
___b. a good student does not want extra help.
___c. a good student thinks extra help is a waste of his time.

5. propel transport

The steam engine was the first engine to __________________ a train.
This sentence means
___a. the steam engine stopped the train.
___b. the steam engine drove the train forward.
___c. the steam engine drove the train backward.

Check your answers with the Key on page 142.

D COMPLETING THE SENTENCES

Choose a word from the box that best completes each sentence. Write it on the line.

transport	repel	confuse	refund
import	impel	refuse	propel

1. The bus will __________________ us to the mall.
2. The car on the lot is a foreign __________________.
3. The smell of garlic will __________________ most people.
4. Poor grades should __________________ you to study harder.
5. If you __________________ to do your job, you could be fired.

Check your answers with the Key on page 142.

E USING THE SKILL

Underline the word that best completes each sentence.

1. Your legs (repel, propel) the bicycle.
2. I need an immediate (refuse, refund) on this ticket.
3. If you (confuse, refuse) someone, that person is puzzled.
4. The government will (deport, import) you if you are not a citizen and commit a crime.
5. The United States will (report, import) many foreign cars this year.

Check your answers with the Key on page 142.

F SUPPLEMENTARY WRITING EXERCISE

The roots that were taught in this lesson are:

-port	-pel	-fuse	-fund

Write sentences in which you use each of the roots in a word in the sentence.

1. ____
2. ____
3. ____
4. ____

A WRITING THE WORDS

A. Write these words on the blank lines. Then say each word.

Write

inscribe	1. ______________
describe	2. ______________
subscribe	3. ______________
transcribe	4. ______________
reserve	5. ______________
conserve	6. ______________
deserve	7. ______________
preserve	8. ______________
inspect	9. ______________
respect	10. ______________

B. Each word contains a word root or word stem. Write the word root or the word stem for each word.

1. ______________
2. ______________
3. ______________
4. ______________
5. ______________
6. ______________
7. ______________
8. ______________
9. ______________
10. ______________

THESE ROOTS OR STEMS HAVE MEANINGS THAT RELATE TO AN **ACTION**.

con-serve \ kən-´serv \ *vt* **con-served; con-serv-ing** [ME *conserven*, fr. MF *conserver*, fr. L. *conservare*, fr. *com-* + *servare* to keep, guard, observe; akin to OE *searu* weapons, armor, Av *haurvaiti* he guards] **1** : to keep in a safe or sound state (he *conserved* and enlarged the estate he inherited); *esp* : to avoid wasteful or destructive use of (~natural resources) **2** : to preserve with sugar **3** : to maintain (a quantity) constant during a process of chemical or physical change ***syn*** see SAVE – **con-serv-er** *n*

in-spect \ in-´spekt \ *vb* [L *inspectus*, pp. of *inspicere*, fr. *in-* + *specere* to look – more at SPY] *vt* **1** : to view closely in critical appraisal : look over **2** : to examine officially <~s the barracks every Friday>~*vi* : to make an inspection ***syn*** see SCRUTINIZE

sub-scribe \ səb-´skrīb \ *vb* **sub-scribed; sub-scrib-ing** [ME *subscriben*, fr. L. *subscribere*, lit., to write beneath, fr. *sub-* + *scribere* to write – more at SCRIBE] *vt* **1** : to write (one's name) underneath : SIGN **2 a** : to sign with one's own hand in token of consent or obligation **b** : to attest by signing **c** : to pledge (a gift or contribution) by writing one's name with the amount **3** : to assent to : SUPPORT *vi* **1** : to sign one's name to a document **2 a** : to give consent or approval to something written by signing <found him unwilling to ~ to the agreement> **b** : to set one's name to a paper in token of promise to give something (as a sum of money); *also* : to give something in accordance with such a promise **c** : to enter one's name for a publication or service; *also* : to receive a periodical or service regularly on order **d** : to agree to purchase and pay for securities esp. of a new offering <*subscribed* for 1000 shares> **3** : to feel favorably disposed <I~ to your sentiments> ***syn*** see ASSENT ***ant*** boggle – **sub-scrib-er** *n*

B USING CONTEXT CLUES

Place an X in front of each correct answer. The word may be used correctly in one or both of the sentences.

1. When you inscribe something,
   ___a. you order it through the mail.
   ___b. you write or engrave something on it.

2. When you describe someone,
   ___a. you write down or say things about that person.
   ___b. you look like that person.

3. When you subscribe to a magazine,
   ___a. you refuse to sign any kind of contract.
   ___b. you agree to purchase the magazine.

4. If a secretary is asked to transcribe a letter,
   ___a. she listens to her boss dictate the letter.
   ___b. she writes or types the letter over.

5. To keep money in reserve means
   ___a. some money is kept aside for emergencies.
   ___b. the money is kept in a safe.

Check your answers with the Key on page 142.

C CHECKING THE MEANING

Read the words in the boxes. Choose the word that best completes the sentence under them. Write that word on the line. Then complete the next sentence by placing an X in front of the correct answer.

1. conserve | deserve

To ensure energy for the future, we must ____________________ energy now.
This sentence means
___a. we must find new sources of energy.
___b. we must save energy.
___c. we must buy more oil from foreign countries.

2. preserve | deserve

Many volunteers ____________________ praise for their unselfish acts.
This sentence means
___a. we must pay volunteers in the future.
___b. many volunteers are selfish.
___c. many volunteers are worthy of praise.

3. preserve | reserve

Wars must sometimes be fought to ____________________ our freedom.
This sentence means
___a. wars help protect and ensure our freedom.
___b. wars do not help us keep our freedom.
___c. wars are the only way to ensure freedom.

4. inspect | respect

The doctor was asked to ____________________ the hospital for cleanliness.
This sentence means
___a. the doctor was asked to close down the hospital.
___b. the doctor praised the hospital for its cleanliness.
___c. the doctor toured the hospital to check its cleanliness.

5. reserve | respect

The boy had a great deal of ____________________ for his father.
This sentence means
___a. the boy looked up to his father.
___b. the boy did not like his father.
___c. the boy was angry with his father.

Check your answers with the Key on page 142.

D COMPLETING THE SENTENCES

Choose a word from the box that best completes each sentence. Write it on the line.

respect	deserve	conserve	describe
inspect	preserve	inscribe	transcribe

1. Children should __________________ their parents.
2. The man wanted to __________________ something special on the bracelet.
3. In the desert, it is necessary to __________________ water.
4. Secretaries are often asked to __________________ letters.
5. Doctors help __________________ the health of their patients.

Check your answers with the Key on page 142.

E USING THE SKILL

Underline the word that best completes each sentence.

1. The girl tried to (describe, inscribe) her new dress to her friend.
2. Many people (inscribe, subscribe) to magazines.
3. Driving at slow speeds helps (reserve, conserve) gas.
4. It is always good to keep some money in (conserve, reserve) for a rainy day.
5. Good grades (describe, deserve) recognition.

Check your answers with the Key on page 142.

F SUPPLEMENTARY WRITING EXERCISE

The roots that were taught in this lesson are:

-scribe	-serve	-spect

Write sentences in which you use each of the roots in a word in the sentence.

1. ____
2. ____
3. ____

A WRITING THE WORDS

A. Write these words on the blank lines. Then say each word.

	Write
provide	1. ______________
inhale	2. ______________
conspire	3. ______________
expire	4. ______________
inspire	5. ______________
exhale	6. ______________
inaudible	7. ______________
provision	8. ______________
auditorium	9. ______________
audience	10. ______________

B. Each word contains a word root or word stem. Write the word root or the word stem for each word.

1. ______________
2. ______________
3. ______________
4. ______________
5. ______________
6. ______________
7. ______________
8. ______________
9. ______________
10. ______________

THESE ROOTS OR STEMS HAVE MEANINGS THAT RELATE TO AN **ACTION** OR TO THE **SENSES**.

au-di-ence \ˈȯd-ē-ən(t)s, ad- \ *n* [ME, fr. L *audentia*, fr. *audient-, audiens,* pp. of *auditre*] **1** : the act or state of hearing **2 a** : a formal hearing or interview <an ~ with the Pope> **b** : an opportunity of being heard <he would succeed if he were once given~> **3 a** : a group of listeners or spectators **b** : the reading public **4** : FOLLOWING <developing an enthusiastic ~ for the free expression of ideas>

in-spire \ in-ˈspī(ə)r \ *vb* **in-spired; in=spir-ing** [ME *inspiren*, fr. MF & L; MF *inspirer*, fr. L *inspirare*, fr. *in-* + *spirare* to breathe – more at SPIRIT] *vt* **1 a** : *archaic* : to breathe or blow into or upon **b** : *archaic* : to infuse (as life) by breathing **2** : INHALE **3 a** : to influence, move, or guide by divine or supernatural inspiration <the gods were believed to ~ the oracles> **b** : to exert an animating, enlivening, or exalting influence on <was particularly *inspired* by the Romanticists> **c** : to spur on : IMPEL, MOTIVATE <threats don't necessarily ~ people to work> **d** : AFFECT <seeing the old room again *inspired* him with nostalgia> **4 a** : to communicate to an agent supernaturally **b** : to draw forth or bring out <thoughts *inspired* his visit to the cathedral> **5 a** : to bring about : OCCASION <the book was *inspired* by his travels>

pro-vide \ prə-ˈvīd \ *vb* **pro-vid-ed; pro-vid-ing** [ME *providen*, fr. L *providēre*, lit., to see ahead, fr. *pro-* forward + *vidēre* to see – more at PRO-, WIT] *vi* **1** : to take precautionary measures <~ for the common defense - *U.S. Constitution*> **2** : to make a proviso or stipulation <the Constitution... ~*s* for an elected two-chamber legislature - *Current Biog.*> **3** : to supply what is needed for sustenance or support <~s for a large family>~*vt* **1** *archaic* : to procure in advance : PREPARE **2 a** : to fit out : EQUIP <~ the children with new shoes> **b** : to supply for use : AFFORD, YIELD <a string quartet *provided* the entertainment> <curtains ~ privacy> **3** : STIPULATE <the contract ~s that the work be completed by a given date>

B USING CONTEXT CLUES

Place an X in front of each correct answer. The word may be used correctly in one or both of the sentences.

1. When you provide something,
   ___a. you cut it into small pieces.
   ___b. you supply what is needed.

2. When you inhale,
   ___a. you breathe in.
   ___b. you breathe out.

3. To conspire means
   ___a. to secretly plan something with another person.
   ___b. to go against what others believe.

4. When something is about to expire,
   ___a. it is growing stronger and stronger.
   ___b. it is coming to an end.

5. When people inspire oxygen, it means
   ___a. they breathe out oxygen.
   ___b. they breathe in oxygen.

Check your answers with the Key on page 142.

C CHECKING THE MEANING

Read the words in the boxes. Choose the word that best completes the sentence under them. Write that word on the line. Then complete the next sentence by placing an X in front of the correct answer.

1. | inhale | | exhale |

When we breathe, we ________________ carbon dioxide.
This sentence means
___a. carbon dioxide is invisible.
___b. carbon dioxide goes out of our lungs.
___c. carbon dioxide goes into our lungs.

2. | inaudible | | provision |

The music from the radio was ________________.
This sentence means
___a. the radio could not be heard.
___b. the radio was too loud.
___c. the radio was broken.

3. | auditorium | | audience |

The man requested an ________________ with the queen.
This sentence means
___a. the man asked the queen for money.
___b. the man asked to be heard by the queen.
___c. the man made an agreement with the queen.

4. | auditorium | | audience |

The meeting was held in the school's ________________.
This sentence means
___a. the meeting was held where no one could hear.
___b. the meeting was held where everyone could hear.
___c. the meeting was held in the classroom.

5. | provide | | provision |

The Red Cross will ________________ you with necessary supplies.
This sentence means
___a. the Red Cross will see that you are safe.
___b. the Red Cross will see that you get what you need.
___c. the Red Cross will not do anything for you.

Check your answers with the Key on page 142.

D COMPLETING THE SENTENCES

Choose a word from the box that best completes each sentence. Write it on the line.

inhale	expire	inaudible	provide
conspire	exhale	audience	auditorium

1. The parking meter was about to ____________________.

2. Be careful not to ____________________ the paint's fumes.

3. After running fast, you ____________________ faster.

4. Parents ____________________ food and shelter for their children.

5. The man's voice was ____________________ because of the loud noise of the passing train.

Check your answers with the Key on page 142.

E USING THE SKILL

Underline the word that best completes each sentence.

1. The Constitution included the (audience, provision) for freedom of speech.

2. It's against the law to (inspire, conspire) against the government.

3. The (audience, auditorium) was sold out for the play's first performance.

4. When you (expire, inspire), you breathe into or upon someone.

5. The (audience, auditorium) clapped when the movie ended.

Check your answers with the Key on page 142.

F SUPPLEMENTARY WRITING EXERCISE

The roots that were taught in this lesson are:

-vide	-spire	-hale	-audi

Write sentences in which you use each of the roots in a word in the sentence.

1. ____

2. ____

3. ____

4. ____

A WRITING THE WORDS

A. Write these words on the blank lines. Then say each word.

	Write
divert	1. ______________
duplicate	2. ______________
convenient	3. ______________
convention	4. ______________
invert	5. ______________
convene	6. ______________
intervene	7. ______________
revert	8. ______________
pervert	9. ______________
implicate	10. ______________

B. Each word contains a word root or root stem. Write the word root or the word stem for each word.

1. ______________
2. ______________
3. ______________
4. ______________
5. ______________
6. ______________
7. ______________
8. ______________
9. ______________
10. ______________

THESE ROOTS OR STEMS HAVE MEANINGS THAT RELATE TO AN **ACTION**.

con-ve-nient \ kən´vēn yənt, -nēənt \ *adj* [ME, fr. L *convenient, conveniens* suitable, pp. of *convenire* to come together, be suitable – more at CONVENE] **1** *obs* **a** : FIT, ADAPTED , SUITABLE, CONGRUOUS <feed me with food ~ for me Prov 30:8 (AV)> **b** : APPROPRIATE, BECOMING, PROPER **2 a** : suited to personal ease or comfort or to easy performance of some act or function <programs broadcast at hours that are more ~ for me>

con-ven-tion \ kən-´ven-chən \ *n* [ME, fr. MF or L; MF, fr. L *convention-, conventio*, fr. *conventus*, pp. of *convenire* to come together, be suitable, fr. *com-* + *venire* to come – more at COME] **1 a** : AGREEMENT, CONTRACT **b** : an agreement between states for regulation of matters affecting all of them **c** : a compact between opposing commanders esp. concerning prisoner exchange or armistice **d** : a general agreement about basic principles; *also* : a principle that is true by convention **2 a** : the summoning or convening of an assembly **b** : an assembly of persons met for a common purpose; *esp* : a meeting of the delegates of a political party for the purpose of formulating a platform and selecting candidates for office **c** : the usu. state or national organization of a religious denomination **3 a** : usage or custom esp. in social matters **b** : a rule of conduct or behavior **c** : a practice in bidding or playing that conveys information between partners in a card game (as bridge) **d** : an established theatrical technique or practice (as a stage whisper or spotlighting)

im-pli-cate \ ´im-plə kāt \ *vt* **-cat-ed; -cat-ing** [L *implicatus*, pp. of *implicare* – more at EMPLOY] **1** : *archaic* : to fold or twist together : ENTWINE **2** : to involve as a consequence, corollary, or natural inference : IMPLY **3 a** : to bring into intimate or incriminating connection **b** : to involve in the nature of operation of something ***syn*** see INVOLVE

re-vert \ ri-´vərt \ *vi* [ME, *reverten*, fr. MF *revertir*, fr. L *reveriere*, v.t., to turn back & *reverti*, v.i., to return, come back, fr. *re-* + *vertere*, *verti* to turn – more at WORTH] **1** : to come or go back esp. to a lower or worse condition <many *~ed* to savagery> **2** : to return to the proprietor or his heirs at the end of a reversion **3** : to return to an ancestral type ***syn*** see RETURN – **re-vert-er** *n* – **re-vert-ible** \ -´vert-e-bel \ *adj.*

B USING CONTEXT CLUES

Place an X in front of each correct answer. The word may be used correctly in one or both of the sentences.

1. To <u>divert</u> something means
   ___a. to turn it around.
   ___b. to change its direction.

2. When you <u>duplicate</u> something,
   ___a. you copy it.
   ___b. you improve it.

3. If something is <u>convenient</u>
   ___a. it's handy.
   ___b. it's a waste of time.

4. When a <u>convention</u> is held,
   ___a. a large group of people come together for a common purpose.
   ___b. it is not necessary to have people attend.

5. When you <u>invert</u> something,
   ___a. you turn it around.
   ___b. you decrease its value.

Check your answers with the Key on page 143.

C CHECKING THE MEANING

Read the words in the boxes. Choose the word that best completes the sentence under them. Write that word on the line. Then complete the next sentence by placing an X in front of the correct answer.

1. convene | intervene

The meeting was about to ________________.
This sentence means
___a. the meeting was about to be cancelled.
___b. the meeting was over.
___c. the meeting was about to begin.

2. intervene | invert

The policeman attempted to ________________ in the fight before anyone got hurt.
This sentence means
___a. the policeman arrested both men.
___b. the policeman tried to break up the fight.
___c. the policeman boycotted the fight.

3. revert | divert

Once released from prison, the man was quick to ________________ to his old ways.
This sentence means
___a. the criminal went back to his old ways.
___b. the criminal never committed another crime.
___c. the criminal became an honest citizen.

4. pervert | revert

The man on trial tried to ________________ the truth.
This sentence means
___a. the man tried to tell the truth.
___b. the man tried to recognize the truth.
___c. the man tried to distort what was true.

5. implicate | duplicate

The policeman tried to ________________ the witness in the crime.
This sentence means
___a. the policeman tried to involve the witness in the crime.
___b. the policeman tried to prove the witness innocent.
___c. the policeman tried to confuse the witness.

Check your answers with the Key on page 143.

D COMPLETING THE SENTENCES

Choose a word from the box that best completes each sentence. Write it on the line.

convene	revert	convention	convenient
duplicate	invert	implicate	divert

1. The Senate will ________________ at approximately 8:00 a.m.
2. Delegates to a political ________________ nominate a candidate.
3. Living near the mall is very ________________.
4. An attempt was made to ________________ the course of the raging river.
5. The employer asked his secretary to ________________ the report.

Check your answers with the Key on page 143.

E USING THE SKILL

Underline the word that best completes each sentence.

1. To empty a wastebasket, it is best to (divert, invert) it.
2. Sometimes people find it hard not to (convene, revert) to bad habits.
3. Always make a (duplicate, convenient) set of car keys.
4. Parents are often forced to (intervene, invert) when their children argue.
5. The teenager tried to (duplicate, implicate) his friends in the robbery.

Check your answers with the Key on page 143.

F SUPPLEMENTARY WRITING EXERCISE

The roots that were taught in this lesson are:

-vene	-vert	-pli

Write sentences in which you use each of the roots in a word in the sentence.

1. ____
2. ____
3. ____

A WRITING THE WORDS

A. Write these words on the blank lines.
Then say each word.

Write

bisect	1. ______________
deflect	2. ______________
predict	3. ______________
intersect	4. ______________
dissect	5. ______________
reflection	6. ______________
contradict	7. ______________
flexible	8. ______________
indicate	9. ______________
reflexes	10. ______________

B. Each word contains a word root or word stem.
Write the word root or the word stem for each word.

1. ______________
2. ______________
3. ______________
4. ______________
5. ______________
6. ______________
7. ______________
8. ______________
9. ______________
10. ______________

THESE ROOTS OR STEMS HAVE MEANINGS THAT RELATE TO AN **ACTION**.

pre-dict \ pri-ˈdikt \ *vb* [L *praedictus*, pp. of *praedicere*, fr. *prae-* pre + *dicere* to say – more at DICTION] *vt* : to declare in advance: *esp* : foretell on the basis of observation, experience, or scientific reason~*vi* : to make a prediction ***syn*** see FORETELL

in-ter-sect \ int-ər-ˈsekt \ *vb* [L *intersectus*, pp. of *intersecare*, fr. *inter-* + *secare* to cut – more at SAW] *vt* : to pierce or divide by passing through or across : CROSS~*vi* **1** : to meet and cross at a point **2** : to share a common area : OVERLAP

re-flect \ ri-ˈflekt \ *vb* [ME *reflecten*, fr. L *reflectere* to bend back, fr. *re-* + *flectere* to bend] *vt* **1** : *archaic* : to turn into or away from a course : DEFLECT **2** : to turn, throw, or bend off or backward at an angle <a mirror ~*s* light> **3** : to bend or fold back **4** : to give back or exhibit as an image, likeness, or outline : MIRROR <the clouds were ~*ed* in the water> **5** : to bring or cast as a result <his attitude ~*s* little credit on his judgment> **6** : to make manifest or apparent : SHOW <the pulse ~*s* the condition of the heart> **7** : REALIZE, CONSIDER *vi* **1** : to throw back light or sound **2 a** : to think quietly and calmly **b** : to express a thought or opinion resulting from reflection **3 a** : to tend to bring reproach or discredit <an investigation that ~*s* on all the members of the department> **b** : to bring about a specified appearance or characterization <an act which ~*s* well on him> **c** : to have a bearing or influence ***syn*** see THINK

B USING CONTEXT CLUES

Place an X in front of each correct answer. The word may be used correctly in one or both of the sentences.

1. To <u>bisect</u> an angle is to
   ___a. make it identical to another angle.
   ___b. divide it into two smaller angles.

2. The soldier used the shield to <u>deflect</u> the bullet means
   ___a. the soldier kept the bullet from striking him.
   ___b. the soldier molded the bullet with his shield.

3. When you <u>predict</u> something,
   ___a. you know about something before it happens.
   ___b. you have no idea what is going to happen.

4. When two streets <u>intersect</u>,
   ___a. they run parallel to one another.
   ___b. they cut across one another.

5. When you <u>dissect</u> something,
   ___a. you cut it into pieces.
   ___b. you copy it exactly.

Check your answers with the Key on page 143.

C CHECKING THE MEANING

Read the words in the boxes. Choose the word that best completes the sentence under them. Write that word on the line. Then complete the next sentence by placing an X in front of the correct answer.

1. dissect   intersect

The biologist will ________________ the frog.
This sentence means
___a. the scientist will cut the frog open and examine it.
___b. the scientist will sew the frog back together.
___c. the scientist will display the frog for his students.

2. reflection   deflect

The girl saw her ________________ in the water.
This sentence means
___a. the girl saw her future in the water.
___b. the girl saw her image in the water.
___c. the girl saw her best friend in the water.

3. contradict   predict

The girl tried to ________________ what her parents had said.
This sentence means
___a. the girl agreed with what her parents had said.
___b. the girl did not agree with her parents.
___c. the girl did not listen to what her parents said.

4. flexible   deflect

The plastic pipe was very ________________.
This sentence means
___a. the plastic pipe was easy to bend.
___b. the plastic pipe was very strong.
___c. the plastic pipe would not melt.

5. indicate   predict

A speedometer will ________________ the speed at which a car is moving.
This sentence means
___a. the speedometer keeps the car moving.
___b. the speedometer has nothing to do with the car.
___c. the speedometer shows the driver how fast the car is going.

Check your answers with the Key on page 143.

D COMPLETING THE SENTENCES

Choose a word from the box that best completes each sentence. Write it on the line.

bisect	contradict	dissect	flexible
intersect	predict	indicate	deflect

1. A cross is formed when two lines ________________.
2. People are ________________ when they are willing to change.
3. To go against what people say means that you ________________ them.
4. Heavy, dark clouds often ________________ that rain is on the way.
5. The scientist tried to ________________ the results of his experiment.

Check your answers with the Key on page 143.

E USING THE SKILL

Underline the word that best completes each sentence.

1. The geometry teacher asked the student to (bisect, dissect) the angle.
2. As people grow older, their (reflexes, bisects) diminish.
3. A mirror can be used to (reflect, bisect) the rays of the sun.
4. Some people believe that a crystal ball can (deflect, predict) one's future.
5. In biology class, students often (intersect, dissect) frogs.

Check your answers with the Key on page 143.

F SUPPLEMENTARY WRITING EXERCISE

The roots that were taught in this lesson are:

-sect	-dict	-flex	-flect

Write sentences in which you use each of the roots in a word in the sentence.

1. ____
2. ____
3. ____
4. ____

A WRITING THE WORDS

A. Write these words on the blank lines.
Then say each word.

Write

doctor	1. ______
sailor	2. ______
conductor	3. ______
teacher	4. ______
waitress	5. ______
actress	6. ______
announcer	7. ______
advisor	8. ______
pianist	9. ______
druggist	10. ______

B. Each word ends in a suffix. Write the suffix for each word.

1. ______
2. ______
3. ______
4. ______
5. ______
6. ______
7. ______
8. ______
9. ______
10. ______

EACH OF THE SUFFIXES RELATES TO A **PERSON** OR **ONE THAT DOES**.

-ess \əs, *also* ˌes \ *n suffix* [ME, *-esse*, fr. OF, fr. LL *-issa*, fr. Gk] : female <gian*tess*>

-ist \əst \ *n suffix* [ME *-iste*, fr. OF & L; OF *-iste*, fr. L *-ista*, *istes*, fr. Gk *-istēs*, fr. verbs in *-izein -ize*] **1 a** : one that performs a (specified) action <cycl*ist*> : one that makes or produces a (specified) thing <novel*ist*> **b** : one that plays a (specified) musical instrument <harp*ist*> **c** : one that operates a (specified) mechanical instrument or contrivance <automobil*ist*> **2** : one that specializes in a (specified) art or science or skill <geolog*ist*> <ventriloqu*ist*> **3** : one that adheres to or advocates a (specified) doctrine or system or code of behavior <social*ist*> <royal*ist*> <hedon*ist*> or that of a (specified) individual <Calvin*ist*> <Darwin*ist*>

[1]**-or** \ ər, ˌȯ(ə)r \ *n suffix* [ME, fr. OF *-eur, -eor* & L *-or*; OF *-eur*, fr. L *-or*; OF *-eor*, fr. L *-ator* or fr. *-atus*, pp. suffix + *-or* – more at -ATE] : one that does a (specified) thing <grant*or*>
[2]**-or** \ər \ *n suffix* [ME, fr. OF *-eur*, fr. L *-or*] : condition : activity <demean*or*>

B USING CONTEXT CLUES

Place an X in front of each correct answer. The word may be used correctly in one or both of the sentences.

1. A doctor is one who
   ___a. helps sick people get well.
   ___b. fixes broken water pipes.

2. A sailor is one who
   ___a. spends time on a train.
   ___b. spends time on a ship.

3. A conductor is one who
   ___a. collects passengers' tickets.
   ___b. leads an orchestra.

4. A teacher is one who
   ___a. writes technical journals.
   ___b. helps people learn.

5. A waitress
   ___a. is a woman who works in a restaurant.
   ___b. is a man who works in a restaurant.

Check your answers with the Key on page 143.

C CHECKING THE MEANING

Read the words in the boxes. Choose the word that best completes the sentence under them. Write that word on the line. Then complete the next sentence by placing an X in front of the correct answer.

1. actress | doctor

The ________________ had a starring role in the movie.
This sentence means
___a. the star was a man.
___b. the star was very famous.
___c. the star was a lady.

2. announcer | advisor

The ________________ helped the student plan the classes he should take.
This sentence means
___a. the student got help from the crossing guard.
___b. the student got help from his mother.
___c. the student was assisted by a knowledgeable person.

3. announcer | pianist

The ________________ played the instrument very well.
This sentence means
___a. the person played the piano well.
___b. the person played the tuba well.
___c. the person played the harmonica well.

4. druggist | announcer

The ________________ filled my prescription.
This sentence means
___a. this person works in a pill factory.
___b. this person can give you what the doctor ordered.
___c. this person always works in a supermarket.

5. announcer | actress

The ________________ worked at the football stadium.
This sentence means
___a. this person tells what is happening during a football game.
___b. this person sells popcorn at the stadium.
___c. this person takes pictures at football games.

Check your answers with the Key on page 143.

D COMPLETING THE SENTENCES

Choose a word from the box that best completes each sentence. Write it on the line.

doctor	sailor	pianist	druggist
teacher	conductor	advisor	actress

1. A __________________ must study many types of diseases.
2. The __________________ gave a concert in the auditorium.
3. The __________________ led the orchestra.
4. The __________________ helped his students find the answers.
5. The woman asked an __________________ for suggestions on how to save money.

Check your answers with the Key on page 143.

E USING THE SKILL

Underline the word that best completes each sentence.

1. The (waitress, actress) won an award for her performance in the drama.
2. The (teacher, doctor) operated on his patient.
3. A (sailor, conductor) uses a compass to chart the course of a ship.
4. The (actress, announcer) worked for a radio station.
5. The (advisor, druggist) gave the lady her prescription.

F SUPPLEMENTARY WRITING EXERCISE

The suffixes that were taught in this lesson are:

-or	-ess	-ist

Write sentences in which you use each of the suffixes in a word in the sentence.

1. ____
2. ____
3. ____

A WRITING THE WORDS

A. Write these words on the blank lines.
Then say each word.

Write

entertainment	1. ______________
development	2. ______________
enlargement	3. ______________
concentration	4. ______________
penetration	5. ______________
regulation	6. ______________
collision	7. ______________
circumference	8. ______________
circumstance	9. ______________
conference	10. ______________

B. Each word ends with a suffix. Write the suffix for each word.

1. ______________
2. ______________
3. ______________
4. ______________
5. ______________
6. ______________
7. ______________
8. ______________
9. ______________
10. ______________

THESE SUFFIXES HAVE MEANINGS THAT RELATE TO AN **ACTION** OR **PROCESS**.

-ence \ ən(t)s, ᵊn(t)s \ *n suffix* [ME, fr. OF, fr. L *-entia*, fr. *-ent*, *-ens*, -ent- + *-ia* *-y*] **1** : action or process <refer*ence*> **2** : quality or state <despon*dence*>

-ance \ən(t)s, n(t)s \ *n suffix* [ME, fr. OF, fr. L *-antia*, fr. *-ant-*, *-ans* -ant + *-ia* *-y*] **1** : action or process <attend*ance*> <deliver*ance*> <further*ance*> : instance of an action or process <appear*ance*> <per*formance*> **2** : quality or state <resembl*ance*> <tem*perance*> : instance of a quality or state <protuber*ance*> **3** : amount or degree <conduct*ance*> <trans*mittance*>

-ion \ˈīən also ˈīˌän \ *n suffix* [ME *-ioun*, *-ion*, fr. OF *-ion*, fr. L *-ion-*, *io*] **1 a** : act or process <val*idation*> **b** : result of an act or process <regulat*ion*> **2** : state or condition <hydrat*ion*>

ment \ mənt; *homographic verbs are* ment *also* mənt, *the latter less often before a syllable-increasing suffix* \ *n suffix* [ME, fr. OF, fr. L *-mentum*; akin to L *-men*, suffix denoting concrete result, Gk *-mat-*, *-ma*] **1 a** : concrete result, object, or agent of a (specified) action <embank*ment*> <entangle*ment*> **b** : concrete means or instrument of a (specified) action <entertain*ment*> **2 a** : action : process <encircle*ment*> <develop*ment*> **b** : place of a (specified) action <encamp*ment*> **3** : state or condition <amaze*ment*> <fulfill*ment*> <involve*ment*>

B USING CONTEXT CLUES

Place an X in front of each correct answer. The word may be used correctly in one or both of the sentences.

1. The play was entertainment means
   ___a. the play was terrible and no one enjoyed it.
   ___b. the play was well done and everyone enjoyed it.

2. Human beings pass through many stages of development means
   ___a. human beings undergo many changes while growing.
   ___b. human beings do not change.

3. The doctor was concerned about the steady enlargement of the bruise means
   ___a. the doctor was concerned about the size of the bruise.
   ___b. the doctor was concerned about the color of the bruise.

4. Some tap water contains a larger concentration of chlorine than needed means
   ___a. some tap water is too strong to drink.
   ___b. high doses of chlorine are found in some water.

5. Penetration of the skin by the needle was difficult means
   ___a. the needle went through the skin easily.
   ___b. the needle went through the skin with some difficulty.

Check your answers with the Key on page 144.

C CHECKING THE MEANING

Read the words in the boxes. Choose the word that best completes the sentence under them. Write that word on the line. Then complete the next sentence by placing an X in front of the correct answer.

1. | regulation | | collision |

The young driver was involved in a ________________.
This sentence means
___a. the young driver saw an accident.
___b. the young driver had an accident.
___c. the young driver had no license.

2. | circumference | | circumstance |

The ________________ of the world is about 25,000 miles.
This sentence means
___a. the distance between the North and South poles is about 25,000 miles.
___b. the distance to the moon is about 25,000 miles.
___c. the distance around the world is about 25,000 miles.

3. | circumstance | | conference |

Under no ________________ should anyone drink poison.
This sentence means
___a. if there is an emergency, you may drink poison.
___b. if lost in the desert with no water, you may drink poison.
___c. poison should never be drunk.

4. | regulation | | penetration |

The ________________ of speeds at which people drive can save gas.
This sentence means
___a. people can only drive as fast as the law allows.
___b. people can travel as fast as they want.
___c. by controlling your car's speed, you will use less gas.

5. | conference | | circumference |

A ________________ was called to discuss the school's budget.
This sentence means
___a. a meeting was called to talk about money.
___b. a tournament was held to raise money for the school.
___c. a convention was held to discuss the school's budget.

Check your answers with the Key on page 144.

D COMPLETING THE SENTENCES

Choose a word from the box that best completes each sentence. Write it on the line.

collision	entertainment	concentration	enlargement
regulation	development	conference	circumstance

1. A clown provided ____________________ at the birthday party.
2. The actual ____________________ of a spacecraft takes many years.
3. Three trains were involved in the ____________________.
4. The picture was an ____________________ of a smaller photo.
5. The ____________________ of sugar in the drink made the drink very sweet.

Check your answers with the Key on page 144.

E USING THE SKILL

Underline the word that best completes each sentence.

1. The deep (regulation, penetration) of the splinter hurt the boy.
2. Four people were hurt as a result of the (conference, collision).
3. The (circumstance, circumference) of the model globe was 25 inches.
4. Many people feel the (penetration, regulation) of energy is unnecessary.
5. Movies provide (development, entertainment) for many people.

Check your answers with the Key on page 144.

F SUPPLEMENTARY WRITING EXERCISE

The suffixes that were taught in this lesson are:

-ment	-ion	-ance	-ence

Write sentences in which you use each of the suffixes in a word in the sentence.

1. ____
2. ____
3. ____
4. ____

A WRITING THE WORDS

A. Write these words on the blank lines. Then say each word.

Write

authority	1. ____________
simplicity	2. ____________
opportunity	3. ____________
weakness	4. ____________
slowness	5. ____________
smoothness	6. ____________
shortness	7. ____________
previous	8. ____________
cautious	9. ____________
wondrous	10. ____________

B. Each word ends with a suffix. Write the suffix for each word.

1. ____________
2. ____________
3. ____________
4. ____________
5. ____________
6. ____________
7. ____________
8. ____________
9. ____________
10. ____________

THESE SUFFIXES HAVE MEANINGS THAT RELATE TO **STATE**, **QUALITY**, OR **CONDITION**.

SEQUENCE 6-23

-ity \ət-ē\ *n suffix* [ME *-ite*, fr. OF or L; OF *-ité*, fr. L *-itat-*, *-itas*, fr. -i- (stem vowel of adjs) + *-tat-*, *-tas* ity; akin to Gk *-tēt-*, *-tēs* -ity] : quality : state : degree <alkalin*ity*> <theatrical*ity*>

-ness \nəs\ *n suffix* [ME *-nes*, fr. OE; akin to OHG *-nissa* -ness] : state : condition : quality : degree <good*ness*>

-ous \əs\ *adj suffix* [ME, partly fr. OF *-ous, -eus, -eux*, fr. L *-osus*; partly fr. L *-us*. nom. sing. masc. ending of many adjectives] **1** : full of : abounding in : having : possessing the qualities of <clamor*ous*> <poison*ous*> **2** : having a valence lower than in compounds or ions with an adjective ending in *-ic* <mercur*ous*>

B USING CONTEXT CLUES

Place an X in front of each correct answer. The word may be used correctly in one or both of the sentences.

1. A father has authority over his children means
   ___a. a father cannot control his children.
   ___b. a father can control his children.

2. The car was known for its simplicity means
   ___a. the car did not have many extras.
   ___b. the car had many expensive extras.

3. The senator took the opportunity to say a few words to the crowd means
   ___a. it was a good time to speak to the crowd.
   ___b. it was not a good time to speak to the crowd.

4. There was a weakness in the athlete's right arm means
   ___a. he could not feel his right arm.
   ___b. he had a loss of strength in his right arm.

5. The slowness of the boy made him late for school means
   ___a. the boy rushed to make it to school on time.
   ___b. the boy took his time getting ready for school.

Check your answers with the Key on page 144.

C CHECKING THE MEANING

Read the words in the boxes. Choose the word that best completes the sentence under them. Write that word on the line. Then complete the next sentence by placing an X in front of the correct answer.

1. smoothness | shortness

Ladies enjoy the ___________________ of a silk dress.
This sentence means
___a. ladies like the color of silk.
___b. ladies like the feeling of silk.
___c. ladies like silk because it is cheap.

2. shortness | previous

The students were surprised by the ___________________ of the test.
This sentence means
___a. the test was too long.
___b. the test was cancelled.
___c. the test was not as long as the students had expected.

3. cautious | previous

The ___________________ owner of the car did not take care of it.
This sentence means
___a. the car was brand-new.
___b. the earlier owner did not take care of the car.
___c. the car was scratched and dented.

4. cautious | wondrous

The Grand Canyon is a ___________________ sight to see.
This sentence means
___a. the Grand Canyon is full of wonder.
___b. the Grand Canyon is not man-made.
___c. the Grand Canyon is a tourist attraction.

5. cautious | previous

The hikers were ___________________ as they walked along the trail.
This sentence means
___a. the hikers were careful.
___b. the hikers were careless.
___c. the hikers were excited.

Check your answers with the Key on page 144.

D COMPLETING THE SENTENCES

Choose a word from the box that best completes each sentence. Write it on the line.

authority	opportunity	slowness	cautious
simplicity	weakness	smoothness	wondrous

1. A foreman has the ________________________ to give orders.
2. The actor was given the ________________________ to play the leading role.
3. Landing on the moon was a ________________________ event for the world.
4. Poor eating habits can cause ________________________ in the body.
5. A ________________________ driver is a safe driver.

Check your answers with the Key on page 144.

E USING THE SKILL

Underline the word that best completes each sentence.

1. The (previous, cautious) senior prom was a huge success.
2. The (smoothness, wondrous) of the flight was enjoyed by the passengers.
3. A surgeon must be very (wondrous, cautious) when he operates.
4. The buyer liked the (slowness, simplicity) of the house.
5. The (slowness, opportunity) of the employee angered his employer.

Check your answers with the Key on page 144.

F SUPPLEMENTARY WRITING EXERCISE

The suffixes that were taught in this lesson are:

-ity	-ness	-ous

Write sentences in which you use each of the suffixes in a word in the sentence.

1. ____
2. ____
3. ____

A WRITING THE WORDS

A. Write these words on the blank lines. Then say each word.

Write

approval	1. ________
vertical	2. ________
horizontal	3. ________
easily	4. ________
cleverly	5. ________
carefully	6. ________
angrily	7. ________
adversary	8. ________
summary	9. ________
planetary	10. ________

B. Each word ends with a suffix. Write the suffix for each word.

1. ________
2. ________
3. ________
4. ________
5. ________
6. ________
7. ________
8. ________
9. ________
10. ________

THESE SUFFIXES MEAN **CHARACTERISTIC OF** OR **PLACE OF**.

[1]-al \ əl, ᵊl \ *adj suffix* [ME, fr. OF & L; OF, fr. L *-alis*] : of, relating to, or characterized by <direction*al*> <fiction*al*>
[2]-al \ " \ *n suffix* [ME *-aille*, fr. OF, fr. L *-alia*, neut. pl. of *-alis*] : action : process <*rehearsal*>
[3]-al \ ˌal, ˌȯl, əl, ᵊl \ *n suffix* [F, fr. *alcool* alcohol, fr. ML *alcohol*] **1** : aldehyde <butan*al*> **2** : acetal <butyr*al*>

[1]-ary \ *US usu* ˌer-ē *when an unstressed syllable precedes,* ə-rē *or* rē *when a stressed syllable precedes; Brit usu* ə-rē or rē *in all cases* \ *n suffix* [ME *-aire*, fr. L *-arius, -aria, -arium*, fr. *-arius*, adj. suffix] **1** : thing belonging to or connected with; *esp* : place of <*ovary*> **2** : person belonging to, connected with, or engaged in <function*ary*>

[2]-ary *adj. suffix* [ME, *-arie*, fr. MF & L; MF *-aire*, fr. L *-arius*] : of, relating to, or connected with <budget*ary*>

[1]-ly \ lē \ *adj suffix* [ME, fr. OE *-līc, -lic*; akin to OHG *-lih;* both fr. a prehistoric Gmc noun represented by OE *lic* body – more at LIKE] **1** : like in appearance, manner, or nature : having the characteristics of <queen*ly*> <father*ly*> **2** : characterized by regular recurrence in (specified) units of time <hour*ly*>
[2]-ly *adv suffix* [ME, fr. OE *-lice, lice*, fr. *-lic*, adj suffix] **1** : in a (specified) manner <slow*ly*> : in the manner of <soldier*ly*> **2** : from a (specified) point of view <eschatological*ly*> **3** : with respect to <part*ly*>

B USING CONTEXT CLUES

Place an X in front of each correct answer. The word may be used correctly in one or both of the sentences.

1. To give your approval means
   ___a. to give a favorable opinion.
   ___b. to give no opinion.

2. If a person is in a vertical position,
   ___a. he is laying down.
   ___b. he is standing.

3. The plane was flying in a horizontal position means
   ___a. the plane was upside down.
   ___b. the plane was level.

4. The student completed his homework easily means
   ___a. the student had no trouble doing his homework.
   ___b. the student finished his homework with difficulty.

5. The child answered his mother cleverly means
   ___a. the child's answer was intelligent.
   ___b. the child's answer made no sense.

Check your answers with the Key on page 144.

C CHECKING THE MEANING

Read the words in the boxes. Choose the word that best completes the sentence under them. Write that word on the line. Then complete the next sentence by placing an X in front of the correct answer.

1. carefully | angrily

The father picked up the new baby ________________.
This sentence means
___a. the father picked up the baby gently.
___b. the father picked up the baby quickly.
___c. the father dropped the baby.

2. summary | adversary

John is Al's ________________ in the race.
This sentence means
___a. both boys are best friends.
___b. both boys are rivals.
___c. both boys are related to each other.

3. planetary | horizontal

The boy was interested in ________________ science.
This sentence means
___a. the boy was interested in animals.
___b. the boy was interested in planets.
___c. the boy was interested in plants.

4. summary | vertical

The history book has a ________________ at the end of each chapter.
This sentence means
___a. the main points of each chapter are listed at the chapter's end.
___b. a test follows each chapter.
___c. a list of authors follow each chapter.

5. angrily | easily

The teenager answered his father ________________.
This sentence means
___a. the teenager was very polite.
___b. the teenager was very worried.
___c. the teenager was very upset.

Check your answers with the Key on page 144.

D COMPLETING THE SENTENCES

Choose a word from the box that best completes each sentence. Write it on the line.

approval	easily	summary	carefully
vertical	cleverly	horizontal	adversary

1. After repairing the door, it opened ________________ and smoothly.
2. A book report is a ________________ of a book you have read.
3. The teacher needs the principal's ________________ to take her class on a field trip.
4. Jack is Bud's ________________ in the spelling competition.
5. The murder mystery was ________________ written.

Check your answers with the Key on page 144.

E USING THE SKILL

Underline the word that best completes each sentence.

1. Another word that means straight up and down is (horizontal, vertical).
2. One must drive (cleverly, carefully) at all times.
3. Teenagers need their school's (vertical, approval) to work after school.
4. The spaceship was used for (summary, planetary) travel.
5. Most people sleep in a (vertical, horizontal) position.

Check your answers with the Key on page 144.

F SUPPLEMENTARY WRITING EXERCISE

The suffixes that were taught in this lesson are:

-al	-ly	-ary

Write sentences in which you use each of the suffixes in a word in the sentence.

1. ____
2. ____
3. ____

A WRITING THE WORDS

A. Write these words on the blank lines. Then say each word.

Write

defective	1. ______________
primitive	2. ______________
classify	3. ______________
modify	4. ______________
dramatize	5. ______________
descriptive	6. ______________
magnify	7. ______________
organize	8. ______________
authorize	9. ______________
attractive	10. ______________

B. Each word ends with a suffix. Write the suffix for each word.

1. ______________
2. ______________
3. ______________
4. ______________
5. ______________
6. ______________
7. ______________
8. ______________
9. ______________
10. ______________

EACH OF THESE SUFFIXES RELATE TO AN **ACTION**.

-fy \ˌfī\ *vb suffix* [ME *-fien*, fr. OF *-fier*, fr. L *-fiacre*, fr. *-ficus* -fic] **1** : make : form into <dandi*fy*> **2** : invest with the attributes of : make similar to <citi*fy*>

-ive \ iv \ *adj suffix* [ME *-if, -ive*, fr. MF & L; MF *-if*, fr. L *-ivus*] : that performs or tends toward an (indicated) action <amus*ive*>

-ize \ˌīz\ *vb suffix* [ME *-isen*, fr. OF *-iser*, fr. LL *-izare*, fr. Gk *-isein*] **1 a** : (1) : cause to be or conform to or resemble <system*ize*> <American*ize*> : cause to be formed into <union*ize*> (2) : subject to a (specified) action <plagiar*ize*> (3) : impregnant or treat or combine with <albumin*ize*> **b** : treat like <idol*ize*> **c** : treat according to the method of <bowdler*ize*> **2 a** : become : become like <crystal*ize*> **b** : be productive in or of <hypothes*ize*> : engage in a (specified) activity <philosoph*ize*> **c** : adopt or spread the manner of activity or the teaching of <calvin*ize*>

B USING CONTEXT CLUES

Place an X in front of each correct answer. The word may be used correctly in one or both of the sentences.

1. The refrigerator was defective means
   ___a. the refrigerator was working correctly.
   ___b. something was wrong with the refrigerator.

2. A primitive people were found on the island means
   ___a. an uncivilized people were found on the island.
   ___b. a civilized people were found on the island.

3. They attempted to classify the flowers by type means
   ___a. they attempted to put the flowers into a vase.
   ___b. they attempted to put the flowers in some order.

4. The boys want to modify the car means
   ___a. the boys want to change the car.
   ___b. the boys want to drive the car.

5. The actors will dramatize the story means
   ___a. the actors will act out the story.
   ___b. the actors will receive an award.

Check your answers with the Key on page 145.

C CHECKING THE MEANING

Read the words in the boxes. Choose the word that best completes the sentence under them. Write that word on the line. Then complete the next sentence by placing an X in front of the correct answer.

1. | defective | | descriptive |

The advertisement was very ____________________ of the product.
This sentence means
___a. the advertisement was poorly written.
___b. the advertisement said little about the product.
___c. the advertisement described the product in detail.

2. | classify | | modify |

The scientist will ____________________ the viruses.
This sentence means
___a. the scientist will kill the viruses.
___b. the scientist will cultivate the viruses.
___c. the scientist will identify the viruses.

3. | modify | | magnify |

A telescope will ____________________ the planets.
This sentence means
___a. a telescope will make the planets appear farther away.
___b. a telescope will make the planets appear nearer.
___c. a telescope will make the planets appear smaller.

4. | organize | | authorize |

A parking permit will ____________________ you to park your car in the parking lot.
This sentence means
___a. you will not be allowed to park your car in the lot.
___b. you will be allowed to exchange your car for another in the lot.
___c. you will be allowed to park your car in the lot.

5. | dramatize | | organize |

An accordion file will help you to ____________________ your papers.
This sentence means
___a. you can file your papers quietly.
___b. you can file your papers quickly.
___c. you can file your papers away neatly.

Check your answers with the Key on page 145.

D COMPLETING THE SENTENCES

Choose a word from the box that best completes each sentence. Write it on the line.

defective	classify	modify	dramatize
primitive	magnify	organize	authorize

1. ___________________ people live off the land without modern conveniences.
2. Someone must ___________________ each car before it can be entered in the exhibit.
3. The Speed Shop can ___________________ your engine to make it go faster.
4. The children will ___________________ the story of Rip Van Winkle.
5. A microbe cannot be seen unless you ___________________ it.

Check your answers with the Key on page 145.

E USING THE SKILL

Underline the word that best completes each sentence.

1. A (descriptive, defective) part caused the washing machine to break down.
2. The researcher worked diligently to (classify, magnify) the new disease.
3. The (descriptive, attractive) woman caught Bill's eye.
4. Susan asked her sister if she would help (organize, dramatize) her room.
5. The landlord will (magnify, modify) the terms of the lease.

Check your answers with the Key on page 145.

F SUPPLEMENTARY WRITING EXERCISE

The suffixes that were taught in this lesson are:

-ive	-fy	-ize

Write sentences in which you use each of the suffixes in a word in the sentence.

1. ____
2. ____
3. ____

A WRITING THE WORDS

A. Write these words on the blank lines. Then say each word.

Write

aimless	1. ____________
lawless	2. ____________
ringlet	3. ____________
graceful	4. ____________
respectful	5. ____________
flawless	6. ____________
bullet	7. ____________
piglet	8. ____________
hopeful	9. ____________
joyful	10. ____________

B. Each word ends with a suffix. Write the suffix for each word.

1. ____________
2. ____________
3. ____________
4. ____________
5. ____________
6. ____________
7. ____________
8. ____________
9. ____________
10. ____________

THESE SUFFIXES HAVE MEANINGS THAT RELATE TO **QUANTITY**, **SIZE**, OR **QUALITY**.

[1]**-ful** \fəl \ *adj suffix sometimes* **-ful-ler** ; *sometimes* **-ful-lest** [ME, fr. OE, fr. *full*, adj] **1** : full of <event*ful*> **2** : characterized by <peace*ful*> **3** : having the qualities of <master*ful*> **4** : -ABLE <mourn*ful*>

[2]**-ful** \ˌfül \ *n suffix* : number of quantity that fills or would fill <room*ful*>

-less \ləs \ *adj suffix* [ME *-les, -lesse*, fr. OE *-lēas*, fr. *-lēas* devoid, false; akin to OGH *lōs* loose, OE *-ˊlosian* to get lost – more at LOSE] **1** : destitute of : not having <wit*less*> <child*less*> **2** : unable to be acted on or to act (in a specified way) <daunt*less*> <fade*less*>

-let \ lət \ *n suffix* [ME, fr. MF *-elet*, fr. *-el*, dim. suffix (fr. L *-eflus*) + *-et*] **1** : small one <book*let*> **2** : article worn <wrist*let*>

B USING CONTEXT CLUES

Place an X in front of each correct answer. The word may be used correctly in one or both of the sentences.

1. The boy's plans for the future were aimless means
   ___a. the boy's plans had direction.
   ___b. the boy's plans were without direction.

2. The Old West was considered to be lawless means
   ___a. the Old West had law and order.
   ___b. the Old West was without law and order.

3. Girls' hair is sometimes styled in ringlets means
   ___a. girls' hair sometimes has large curls.
   ___b. girls' hair sometimes has small curls.

4. The ballet dancer gave a graceful performance means
   ___a. the ballet dancer gave a performance that was filled with movement.
   ___b. the ballet dancer gave a beautiful performance.

5. A person should be respectful toward old people means
   ___a. a person should be full of consideration toward old people.
   ___b. a person should be full of gratitude toward old people.

Check your answer with the Key on page 145.

C CHECKING THE MEANING

Read the words in the boxes. Choose the word that best completes the sentence under them. Write that word on the line. Then complete the next sentence by placing an X in front of the correct answer.

1. aimless | flawless

The completed house was ___________________.
This sentence means
___a. the house had many things wrong with it.
___b. the house had few things wrong with it.
___c. the house had nothing wrong with it.

2. bullet | piglet

The ___________________ would not leave its mother.
This sentence means
___a. the large pig would not leave its mother.
___b. the small pig would leave its mother.
___c. the small pig would not leave its mother.

3. graceful | hopeful

The dancer was very ___________________.
This sentence means
___a. the dancer could not dance well.
___b. the dancer made smooth movements.
___c. the dancer made many movements.

4. ringlet | bullet

The ___________________ hit the target.
This sentence means
___a. the small ball hit the target.
___b. the cannon ball hit the target.
___c. the cannon ball did not hit the target.

5. respectful | hopeful

The doctor was ___________________ that the operation would be a success.
This sentence means
___a. the doctor was sad.
___b. the doctor was filled with anger.
___c. the doctor was filled with hope.

Check your answers with the Key on page 145.

D COMPLETING THE SENTENCES

Choose a word from the box that best completes each sentence. Write it on the line.

aimless	ringlet	graceful	respectful
flawless	bullet	joyful	hopeful

1. The __________________ girl sang and whistled.
2. Many diamonds are __________________.
3. His trip had no direction and was __________________.
4. The young girl was __________________ toward old people.
5. The baby had a __________________ on top of his head.

Check your answers with the Key on page 145.

E USING THE SKILL

Underline the word that best completes each sentence.

1. The (flawless, lawless) town had much crime.
2. The (aimless, flawless) diamond was blue.
3. The (joyful, hopeful) girl wished for success.
4. The (bullet, ringlet) found its target.
5. The (respectful, graceful) swans headed down the river.

Check your answers with the Key on page 145.

F SUPPLEMENTARY WRITING EXERCISE

The suffixes that were taught in this lesson are:

-less	-let	-ful

Write sentences in which you use each of the suffixes in a word in the sentence.

1. ____
2. ____
3. ____

A WRITING THE WORDS

A. Write these words on the blank lines. Then say each word.

Write

rejected	1. ____________
dejected	2. ____________
observatory	3. ____________
factory	4. ____________
decorator	5. ____________
laboratory	6. ____________
directory	7. ____________
demonstrator	8. ____________
indicator	9. ____________
admitted	10. ____________

B. Each word ends with a suffix. Write the suffix for each word.

1. ____________
2. ____________
3. ____________
4. ____________
5. ____________
6. ____________
7. ____________
8. ____________
9. ____________
10. ____________

THESE SUFFIXES HAVE MEANINGS OF **PLACE**, **ONE THAT DOES**, OR **CHARACTERIZED BY**.

-a-tor \ˌādə(r), ˌātə(r) *sometimes* ˌā ˈtȯ(ə)r *or* ˌtȯ(ə) \ *n suffix* [ME *-atour*, fr. OF & L; OF, fr. L *-ator*, fr. *-atus* -ate + *or*] : one that does <totaliz*ator*>

-ed *vb suffix* [ME *-ede, -de*, fr. OE *-de, -ede, -ode, -ade*; akin to OHG *-ta*, past ending (1st sing.) and prob. to OHG *-t,* pp. ending] – used to form the past tense of regular weak verbs <judg*ed*> <deni*ed*> <dropp*ed*>

-ory *adj suffix* [ME *-orie*, fr. MF & L; MF, fr. L *-orius*] **1** : of, relating to, or characterized by <gustat*ory*> **2** : serving for, producing, or maintaining <justificat*ory*>

B USING CONTEXT CLUES

Place an X in front of each correct answer. The word may be used correctly in one or both of the sentences.

1. The inspector rejected the broken toy means
   ___a. the inspector would not accept the broken toy.
   ___b. the inspector would accept the broken toy.

2. The student felt dejected over his failing grade means
   ___a. the student felt good about his failing grade.
   ___b. the student felt sad about his failing grade.

3. An observatory is a place where one can
   ___a. look at the stars.
   ___b. get some fine food.

4. A factory is a place where
   ___a. one does research.
   ___b. something is manufactured.

5. A decorator is someone who
   ___a. builds hospitals.
   ___b. selects colors.

Check your answers with the Key on page 145.

C CHECKING THE MEANING

Read the words in the boxes. Choose the word that best completes the sentence under them. Write that word on the line. Then complete the next sentence by placing an X in front of the correct answer.

1. rejected | dejected

The foreman ________________ the lumber for the house.
This sentence means
___a. the foreman used the lumber.
___b. the foreman did not use the lumber.
___c. the foreman painted the lumber.

2. observatory | laboratory

A ________________ is a place where new products are developed.
This sentence means
___a. new products are developed in a studio.
___b. new products are developed in a store.
___c. new products are made in a scientific room.

3. factory | directory

I found your number in the ________________.
This sentence means
___a. I found your number in a store.
___b. I found your number in a recipe.
___c. I found your number in a book.

4. demonstrator | indicator

The ________________ showed us the features of the new product.
This sentence means
___a. someone pointed out the features of the new product to us.
___b. someone showed us how to examine the new product.
___c. someone told us how to buy the new product.

5. admitted | dejected

The woman was ________________ to the hospital with a broken hip.
This sentence means
___a. the woman left the hospital with a broken hip.
___b. the woman entered and stayed in the hospital.
___c. the woman visited the hospital.

Check your answers with the Key on page 145.

D COMPLETING THE SENTENCES

Choose a word from the box that best completes each sentence. Write it on the line.

rejected	observatory	indicator	factory
dejected	laboratory	directory	demonstrator

1. The ________________ had a 16-inch telescope for looking at the stars.
2. The minister's address can be found in the church ________________.
3. A place where television sets are made is called a ________________.
4. The dentist said that cavities are an ________________ of poor oral hygiene.
5. In a ________________, chemicals are used for research on new products.

Check your answers with the Key on page 145.

E USING THE SKILL

Underline the word that best completes each sentence.

1. A patient in a hospital is sometimes (rejected, dejected).
2. The chemist worked in a (laboratory, observatory), trying to perfect the drug.
3. New cars are assembled in a (observatory, factory).
4. I would like my office designed by a professional (demonstrator, decorator).
5. A (decorator, demonstrator) will show you how the machine works.

Check your answers with the Key on page 145.

F SUPPLEMENTARY WRITING EXERCISE

The suffixes that were taught in this lesson are:

-ed	-ory	-ator

Write sentences in which you use each of the suffixes in a word in the sentence.

1. ____
2. ____
3. ____

A WRITING THE WORDS

A. Write these words on the blank lines.
Then say each word.

Write

acreage	1. ____________
percentage	2. ____________
courage	3. ____________
multitude	4. ____________
magnitude	5. ____________
altitude	6. ____________
fracture	7. ____________
exposure	8. ____________
lecture	9. ____________
manufacture	10. ____________

B. Each word ends with a suffix. Write the suffix for each word.

1. ____________
2. ____________
3. ____________
4. ____________
5. ____________
6. ____________
7. ____________
8. ____________
9. ____________
10. ____________

THESE SUFFIXES HAVE MEANINGS THAT RELATE TO **CONDITION** OR **PROCESS**.

SEQUENCE 6-28

-age \ ij \ *n suffix* [ME, fr. OF, fr. L *-aticum*] **1** : aggregate : collection <track*age*> **2 a** : action : process <haul*age*> **b** : cumulative result of <break*age*> **c** : rate of <dos*age*> **3** : house or place of <orphan*age*> **4** : state : rank <peon*age*> **5** : fee : charge <post*age*>

-tude \ t(y)üd \ *n suffix* [MF or L; MF, fr. L *-tudin, -tudo*] : NESS <plenti*tude*>

-ure \ə(r), ˌ(y)u̇(ə)r, -u̇ə\ *n suffix* [ME, fr. OF, fr. L *-ura*] **1** : act : process <expos*ure*> **2** : office : function; *also* : body performing (such) function <legisla*ture*>

B USING CONTEXT CLUES

Place an X in front of each correct answer. The word may be used correctly in one or both of the sentences.

1. The farmer planted his <u>acreage</u> in corn means
   ___a. the farmer planted corn in patio pots.
   ___b. the farmer planted corn on his land.

2. He received a <u>percentage</u> of the winnings means
   ___a. he received part of the winnings.
   ___b. he received none of the winnings.

3. The man had a great deal of <u>courage</u> means
   ___a. the man was not afraid of many things.
   ___b. the man was afraid of everything.

4. A <u>multitude</u> of people attended the concert means
   ___a. a great many people attended the concert.
   ___b. a small group of people attended the concert.

5. The <u>magnitude</u> of something
   ___a. is its size.
   ___b. is its color.

Check your answers with the Key on page 146.

C CHECKING THE MEANING

Read the words in the boxes. Choose the word that best completes the sentence under them. Write that word on the line. Then complete the next sentence by placing an X in front of the correct answer.

1. altitude | magnitude

The plane was flying at an __________________ of 30,000 feet.
This sentence means
___a. the plane was 30,000 feet above the ground.
___b. the plane was going 30,000 miles an hour.
___c. the flight was very smooth.

2. fracture | exposure

Too much __________________ to the sun's rays will cause one to sunburn.
This sentence means
___a. it is not a good idea to use suntan lotion.
___b. being in the sun too long can cause one to sunburn.
___c. a sunburn may cause pain.

3. lecture | fracture

The __________________ in the boy's arm was painful.
This sentence means
___a. the boy had scratched his arm.
___b. the boy had an infection in his arm.
___c. the boy had cracked a bone in his arm.

4. lecture | manufacture

The new company president wants to __________________ swimming pools.
This sentence means
___a. the new president wants to repair swimming pools.
___b. the new president wants to build swimming pools.
___c. the new president wants to design swimming pools.

5. lecture | exposure

The teacher prepared a __________________ for the class.
This sentence means
___a. the teacher prepared a test for the class.
___b. the teacher prepared a speech for the class.
___c. the teacher prepared a surprise for the class.

Check your answers with the Key on page 146.

D COMPLETING THE SENTENCES

Choose a word from the box that best completes each sentence. Write it on the line.

acreage	courage	magnitude	exposure
percentage	multitude	altitude	fracture

1. There was one ________________ left in the camera.
2. The ________________ for sale included two miles of oceanfront land.
3. The higher the ________________, the colder the air in space.
4. A bone ________________ is very painful.
5. The ________________ of the space program is hard to imagine.

Check your answers with the Key on page 146.

E USING THE SKILL

Underline the word that best completes each sentence.

1. A (percentage, multitude) of people crowded the circus tent.
2. Firefighters have a great deal of (percentage, courage).
3. The (altitude, lecture) was very long and very boring.
4. Companies (fracture, manufacture) many kinds of products.
5. A small (magnitude, percentage) of the class failed the test.

Check your answers with the Key on page 146.

F SUPPLEMENTARY WRITING EXERCISE

The suffixes that were taught in this lesson are:

-age	-tude	-ure

Write sentences in which you use each of the suffixes in a word in the sentence.

1. ____
2. ____
3. ____

A WRITING THE WORDS

A. Write these words on the blank lines. Then say each word.

Write

candidate	1. ______
participate	2. ______
isolate	3. ______
portable	4. ______
perishable	5. ______
manageable	6. ______
disagreeable	7. ______
classic	8. ______
domestic	9. ______
fantastic	10. ______

B. Each word ends with a suffix. Write the suffix for each word.

1. ______
2. ______
3. ______
4. ______
5. ______
6. ______
7. ______
8. ______
9. ______
10. ______

THESE SUFFIXES MEAN **CHARACTERISTIC OF**, OR **CAPABLE OF**, OR **ONE WHO ACTS**.

-able *also* **-ible** \ə-bəl \ *adj suffix* [ME, fr. OF, fr. L *-abilis, -ibilis*, fr. *-a-*, *-i-*, verb stem vowels + *-bilis* capable or worthy of] **1** : capable of, fit for, or worthy of (being so acted upon or toward) – chiefly in adjectives derived from verbs <break*able*> <collect*ible*> **2** : tending, given, or liable to <knowledge*able*> <perish*able*>

[1]-ate \ət, ˌāt \ *n suffix* [ME, *-at*, fr. OF, fr. L *-atus, -atum*, masc. & neut. of *-atus*, pp. ending] **1** : one acted upon (in a specified way) <distill*ate*> **2** : [NL *-atum*, fr. L] : chemical compound or complex anion derived from a (specified) compound or element <phenol*ate*> <ferr*ate*>; *esp* : salt or ester of an acid with a name ending in *-ic* and not beginning with *hydro-* <bor*ate*>
[2]ate *n suffix* [ME *-at*, fr. OF, fr. L *-atus*, fr. *-atus*, pp. ending] : office : function : rank : group of persons holding a (specified) office or rank or having a (specified) function <vicar*ate*>
[3]ate *adj suffix* [ME *-at*, fr. L *-atus*, fr. pp. ending of 1st conj. verbs, fr. *-a-*, stem vowel of 1st conj. + *-tus*, pp. suffix – more at -ED] : marked by having <crani*ate*>

[4]ate \ˌāt \ *vb suffix* [ME *-aten*, fr. L *-atus*, pp. ending] : act on (in a specified way) <insul*ate*> : cause to be modified or affected by <camphor*ate*> : cause to become <activ*ate*> : furnish with <capacit*ate*>

[1]-ic \ik \ *adj suffix* [ME, fr. OF & L; OF *-igue*, fr. L *-icus* – more at -Y] **1** : having the character or form of : being <panoram*ic*> : consisting of <run*ic*> **2 a** : of or relating to <alderman*ic*> **b** : related to, derived from, or containing <alcohol*ic*> <ole*ic*> **3** : in the manner of : like that of : characteristic of <Byron*ic*> **4** : associated or dealing with <Ved*ic*> : utilizing <electron*ic*> **5** : characterized by : exhibiting <nostalg*ic*> : affected with <aller*gic*> **6** : caused by <amoeb*ic*> **7** : ending to produce compounds or ions named with an adjective ending in *-ous* <ferr*ic* iron>
[2]-ic *n suffix* : one having the character or nature of : one belonging to or associated with : one exhibiting or affected by <glycon*ic*> : one that produces <ecbol*ic*>

B USING CONTEXT CLUES

Place an X in front of each correct answer. The word may be used correctly in one or both of the sentences.

1. A candidate is one who
   ___a. seeks an office.
   ___b. always loses elections.

2. To participate in something means
   ___a. to ignore it.
   ___b. to take part in it.

3. To isolate means
   ___a. to be surrounded by others.
   ___b. to be set apart from others.

4. If something is portable,
   ___a. it can be easily moved.
   ___b. it is very hard to move.

5. If something is perishable,
   ___a. it will spoil easily.
   ___b. it will keep forever.

Check your answers with the Key on page 146.

C CHECKING THE MEANING

Read the words in the boxes. Choose the word that best completes the sentence under them. Write that word on the line. Then complete the next sentence by placing an X in front of the correct answer.

1. | manageable | | disagreeable |

The model's hair is very __________________.
This sentence means
___a. the model's hair is easy to control.
___b. the model's hair looks beautiful.
___c. the model's hair is hard to comb.

2. | disagreeable | | classic |

The old car was a __________________ model.
This sentence means
___a. the car was very run down.
___b. the car was very expensive.
___c. the car was an excellent model of its kind.

3. | domestic | | fantastic |

A cat is a __________________ animal.
This sentence means
___a. a cat is a wild animal.
___b. a cat is a household pet.
___c. a cat is a rare animal.

4. | disagreeable | | perishable |

The old man was very loud and __________________.
This sentence means
___a. the old man was very unpleasant.
___b. the old man was very pleasant.
___c. the old man was very rich.

5. | portable | | fantastic |

A mother read her little boy a __________________ story.
This sentence means
___a. a mother read her son a long story.
___b. a mother read her son a short story.
___c. a mother read her son an imaginative story.

Check your answers with the Key on page 146.

D COMPLETING THE SENTENCES

Choose a word from the box that best completes each sentence. Write it on the line.

isolate	candidate	perishable	disagreeable
classic	portable	participate	manageable

1. When people are tired, they are often ______________________.
2. In hot weather, fruit can become very ____________________.
3. The exceptional employee was a ____________________ for a raise.
4. To really enjoy sports, one must __________________ in them.
5. The book was a __________________ piece of writing.

Check your answers with the Key on page 146.

E USING THE SKILL

Underline the word that best completes each sentence.

1. Doctors often (participate, isolate) very ill patients.
2. The movie had a (domestic, fantastic) ending.
3. The television was a (domestic, portable) model.
4. The car was a (classic, candidate) model.
5. The lion was very (manageable, disagreeable) after he was fed.

Check your answers with the Key on page 146.

F SUPPLEMENTARY WRITING EXERCISE

The suffixes that were taught in this lesson are:

-ate	-able	-ic

Write sentences in which you use each of the suffixes in a word in the sentence.

1. ____
2. ____
3. ____

A WRITING THE WORDS

A. Write these words on the blank lines. Then say each word.

	Write
politician	1. ______________
electrician	2. ______________
beautician	3. ______________
pediatrician	4. ______________
mechanism	5. ______________
criticism	6. ______________
capitalism	7. ______________
feverish	8. ______________
childish	9. ______________
cherish	10. ______________

B. Each word ends with a suffix. Write the suffix for each word.

1. ______________
2. ______________
3. ______________
4. ______________
5. ______________
6. ______________
7. ______________
8. ______________
9. ______________
10. ______________

THESE SUFFIXES MEAN **ONE WHO DOES**, OR SHOWS **RELATIONSHIP** OR **AN ACTION**.

-i-cian \ ˈish-ən \ *n suffix* [ME, fr. OF *-icien*, fr. L *-ica* (as in *rhetorica* rhetoric) + OF *-ien -ian*] : specialist : practitioner <beaut*ician*>

-ish \ ish \ *adj suffix* [ME, fr. OE *-isc*; akin to OHG *-isc, -ish*, Gk *-iskos*, dim. suffix] **1** : of, relating to, or being – chiefly in adjectives indicating nationality or ethnic group <Finn*ish*> **2 a** : characteristic of <boy*ish*> <mul*ish*> **b** (1) : having a touch or trace of <summer*ish*>; somewhat <purpl*ish*> (2) : having the approximate age of <forty*ish*> (3) : being or occurring at the approximate time of <eight*ish*>

-ism \ ˌiz-əm \ *n suffix* [ME *-isme*, fr. MF & L; MF, partly fr. L *-isma* (fr. Gk) & partly fr. L *-ismus*, fr. Gk *-ismos*; Gk *-isma* & *-ismos*, fr. verbs in *-izein -ize*] **1 a** : act : practice : process <critic*ism*> <plagia*rism*> **b** : manner or action or behavior characteristic of a (specified) person or thing <animal*ism*> **2 a** : state : condition : property <barbarian*ism*> **b** : abnormal state or condition resulting from excess of a (specified) thing <alcohol*ism*> or marked by resemblance to (such) a person or thing <mongol*ism*> **3 a** : doctrine : theory : cult <Buddh*ism*> **b** : adherence to a system or a class of principles <stoic*ism*> **4** : characteristic or peculiar feature or trait <colloquial*ism*>

B USING CONTEXT CLUES

Place an X in front of each correct answer. The word may be used correctly in one or both of the sentences.

1. A politician is one who is involved in
   ___a. the affairs of people.
   ___b. some form of government.

2. An electrician is one who works with
   ___a. energy.
   ___b. electricity.

3. A beautician is one who is concerned about
   ___a. appearance.
   ___b. lawns.

4. A pediatrician is one who is concerned about
   ___a. old people.
   ___b. children.

5. A mechanism is
   ___a. a man who fixes machines.
   ___b. a system of parts working together.

Check your answers with the Key on page 146.

C CHECKING THE MEANING

Read the words in the boxes. Choose the word that best completes the sentence under them. Write that word on the line. Then complete the next sentence by placing an X in front of the correct answer.

1. | criticism | | capitalism |

The old man was known to offer __________________ about everything.
This sentence means
___a. the old man liked everything.
___b. the old man found something wrong with everything.
___c. the old man talked all the time.

2. | capitalism | | feverish |

The sick child was __________________.
This sentence means
___a. the sick child was very crabby.
___b. the sick child's temperature was higher than normal.
___c. the sick child's temperature was lower than normal.

3. | childish | | cherish |

Most people have a possession they __________________.
This sentence means
___a. most people own something they dislike.
___b. most people own something they respect.
___c. most people own something they are fond of.

4. | capitalism | | criticism |

An economic system based on a free market is called __________________.
This sentence means
___a. people can buy, sell and trade.
___b. the government dictates what can be bought and sold.
___c. the government owns factories.

5. | childish | | cherish |

Sometimes an adult will act __________________.
This sentence means
___a. sometimes an adult will act like a child.
___b. sometimes an adult will act very dignified.
___c. sometimes an adult will act very mature.

Check your answers with the Key on page 146.

D COMPLETING THE SENTENCES

Choose a word from the box that best completes each sentence. Write it on the line.

politician	beautician	pediatrician	feverish
electrician	mechanism	criticism	childish

1. The clock's ________________ is broken and now it won't work.
2. The ________________ decided to run for state senator.
3. Many people become ________________ when they are ill.
4. The ________________ ran wires under the ground.
5. The moviegoer offered nothing but ________________ for the movie.

Check your answers with the Key on page 146.

E USING THE SKILL

Underline the word that best completes each sentence.

1. The (pediatrician, beautician) cut and curled the girl's hair.
2. When angry, the man acted in a (feverish, childish) way.
3. America is a country that practices (mechanism, capitalism).
4. The (beautician, pediatrician) worked in the children's ward.
5. Husbands and wives should (criticism, cherish) one another.

Check your answers with the Key on page 146.

F SUPPLEMENTARY WRITING EXERCISE

The suffixes that were taught in this lesson are:

-ician	-ish	-ism

Write sentences in which you use each of the suffixes in a word in the sentence.

1. ____
2. ____
3. ____

G SENTENCES FOR SPELLING EXERCISE

SEQUENCE 6-1

1. The entire team was present except for the captain.
2. The crowd was forced to exit the auditorium through the rear door.
3. The exhaust fumes coming from the car had a peculiar odor.
4. To find the difference between two numbers, you must subtract.
5. The submarine's crew could hardly wait to be back on dry land.
6. The divers had to descend to a depth of 150' to locate the cable.
7. The class listened in order to derive as much as possible from lectures.
8. The witness did his best to describe the bank robber accurately.
9. The homes in our subdivision border a man-made lake.
10. It is best to deposit large sums of money in the bank.

G SENTENCES FOR SPELLING EXERCISE

SEQUENCE 6-2

1. Ron failed the class because his work was always incomplete.
2. When looking for factual information, look in the nonfiction section of the library.
3. The painting took first prize because it was very unusual.
4. The professor used a large rock as an example of a nonliving thing.
5. "I've had enough of your nonsense," said the teacher to the bully.
6. The judge was uncertain as to what verdict the jury would deliver.
7. Advertising agencies often use uncommon methods to sell products.
8. A teenager looks forward to becoming an independent adult.
9. The little boy liked to pretend that he was invisible.
10. The man became unconscious after falling down and hitting his head.

G SENTENCES FOR SPELLING EXERCISE

SEQUENCE 6-3

1. The <u>circumference</u> of the circle was 60 inches.
2. The <u>circumstances</u> surrounding the accident were not clear.
3. Magellan's voyage is an example of <u>circumnavigation</u> at sea.
4. A strict <u>program</u> of daily exercise will improve personal health.
5. The ship was making slow <u>progress</u> due to a damaged engine.
6. The science <u>project</u> was almost ready for the annual Science Fair.
7. Immunizations <u>protect</u> us from disease.
8. Coffee must <u>percolate</u> in order to ensure good flavor.
9. The ballet dancer wanted to <u>perform</u> in spite of a broken toe.
10. Things are not always as we <u>perceive</u> them to be.

G SENTENCES FOR SPELLING EXERCISE

SEQUENCE 6-4

1. The secretary added a <u>postscript</u> to the end of the letter.
2. They had to <u>postpone</u> their vacation due to bad weather.
3. <u>Postwar</u> Germany was left in a state of economic ruin.
4. Heavy rain will often <u>precede</u> a hurricane.
5. Driving defensively can <u>prevent</u> an accident.
6. The fortuneteller claims she can <u>predict</u> the future.
7. The car's engine needed to be <u>rebuilt</u>.
8. The factory will <u>recall</u> certain cars to correct a defect in the breaking system.
9. A mirror will <u>reflect</u> the sun's rays.
10. It is sometimes difficult to <u>remember</u> important dates.

G SENTENCES FOR SPELLING EXERCISE

SEQUENCE 6-5

1. A bicycle can be an expensive investment.
2. Onions are a biennial plant.
3. The biplane was flown during the early years of aviation.
4. The monoplane was utilized during World War II.
5. The disc jockey kept up a continuous monologue during the show.
6. Long speeches often become monotonous for the audience.
7. The hospital requires nurses to wear a uniform while on duty.
8. The United States is comprised of fifty individual states.
9. I will attend a university when I graduate from high school.
10. The class answered the teacher's question in unison.

G SENTENCES FOR SPELLING EXERCISE

SEQUENCE 6-6

1. The work done by the plumber was of superior quality.
2. The boy wished that he had superhuman strength with which to fight the bully.
3. A wide range of products is available at your local supermarket.
4. The pilot suffered multiple injuries when his biplane crashed.
5. A liquid is a multiform substance.
6. The actor was surrounded by a multitude of fans.
7. The gun was semiautomatic.
8. The teacher sat the children in a semicircle, then read them a story.
9. The town's semiannual stock-car race begins on Saturday at 10:00 a.m.
10. The semiskilled worker found it difficult to find work.

G SENTENCES FOR SPELLING EXERCISE

SEQUENCE 6-7

1. The scientist attempted to discover an antidote for the poison.
2. An antiseptic was used to cleanse the man's wound.
3. The protesters showed great antipathy toward the war.
4. A word with an opposite meaning is called an antonym.
5. The bombing was an attempt to counteract the enemy's invasion.
6. The antibiotic cured the girl's infection.
7. The opposing party filed a counterclaim to the inheritance.
8. The General needed an effective counterplot to ensure a victory.
9. Be sure not to enter a foreign country carrying contraband items.
10. Witnesses often contradict themselves when testifying.

G SENTENCES FOR SPELLING EXERCISE

SEQUENCE 6-8

1. Wise shoppers compare prices before purchasing a product.
2. Musicians often compose their own musical scores.
3. The Olympics gives athletes the chance to compete internationally.
4. The machine will compress the cans in order to recycle them.
5. Many airline companies do not offer international flights.
6. Many people believe that, one day, interplanetary travel will be commonplace.
7. More regulations are needed to govern interstate commerce.
8. Cards are often used to express sympathy to others.
9. Many people buy season tickets for symphony performances.
10. A Thesaurus is a good source for locating a word's synonym.

G SENTENCES FOR SPELLING EXERCISE

SEQUENCE 6-9

1. Immunizations help to prevent diseases from reaching epidemic numbers.
2. The epidermis is the outer layer of skin.
3. The man will engrave a special message on his girlfriend's ring.
4. The police officers planned to encircle the bank, trapping the robber.
5. Poor firearm technique can endanger the lives of others.
6. The starfish was preparing to envelop the scallop.
7. Be sure to enclose a check when paying a bill by mail.
8. Intrastate commerce is not as profitable as interstate commerce.
9. Intramural sports are played by students attending the same school.
10. The doctor ordered an intravenous medication for his patient.

G SENTENCES FOR SPELLING EXERCISE

SEQUENCE 6-10

1. Important messages were once sent by means of the telegraph.
2. Long-distance telephone conversations can be very expensive.
3. Many people think children watch too much television.
4. Do you believe in the power of mental telepathy?
5. The electron microscope was a magnificent invention.
6. The tape recorder was of no use because the microphone was missing.
7. A microbe is a very tiny living particle.
8. A microwave oven cuts cooking time in half.
9. The king lived in a magnificent castle overlooking the ocean.
10. The lens magnified the size of the cell five times.

G SENTENCES FOR SPELLING EXERCISE

SEQUENCE 6-11

1. The doctor asked the nurse to inject the patient with penicillin.
2. Teenagers often reject their parents' advice.
3. Dirty clothes detract from someone's overall appearance.
4. When you subtract, you take the smaller number away from the larger.
5. The newspaper was forced to retract the girl's story.
6. The priest asked the man to remit his offering by mail.
7. The prisoner was forced to submit to the requests of the guard.
8. Sometimes it's hard to admit your mistakes.
9. Hospital rules will permit only two visitors at a time.
10. If you commit a crime, you may go to jail.

G SENTENCES FOR SPELLING EXERCISE

SEQUENCE 6-12

1. Shoes and purses were made in the Baker Brother's factory.
2. The owner of the plant decided to manufacture perfume and soap.
3. The writer wrote a factual report on the war.
4. The principal decided to suspend the tardy boy for one week.
5. When starting a new business, it is necessary to expend money.
6. The graph would be found in the appendix of the report.
7. Employers like to hire people they can depend on.
8. Be sure to include your return address when addressing an envelope.
9. We will conclude our broadcast by playing the national anthem.
10. The coach had to exclude two athletes from the State Meet.

G SENTENCES FOR SPELLING EXERCISE

SEQUENCE 6-13

1. Deposit large sums of money in the bank as soon as possible.
2. From his position in the bleachers, the man could see the entire field.
3. My neighbor will consider my proposition to mow his lawn for a reasonable fee.
4. The restaurant overlooks the city and revolves in a circle.
5. The producer hoped the new comedy show would evolve into a series.
6. The witness did not want to involve himself in the crime.
7. The teacher hoped her students would resolve the argument.
8. The landlord told his tenants that he wanted to dissolve their lease.
9. Water is a well-known solvent.
10. After his grandmother died, Johnny managed the disposition of her property.

G SENTENCES FOR SPELLING EXERCISE

SEQUENCE 6-14

1. A strict diet and regular exercise can help you retain a youthful shape.
2. The starlet hoped to obtain fame and fortune.
3. Firefighters made a desperate effort to contain the fire.
4. The General was forced to demote the soldier for his actions.
5. It is said that women show more emotion than men.
6. The boys want to exclude all girls from becoming members of their bike club.
7. There will be a musical prelude to the evening's award ceremony.
8. The music offered a brief interlude for the tense audience.
9. The speaker asked for donations as a postlude to his speech.
10. The child attempted to delude his parents with a lie.

G SENTENCES FOR SPELLING EXERCISE

SEQUENCE 6-15

1. The infection made little progress because it was slowed down by the antibiotic.
2. The condition of the house continued to regress with time.
3. Too often a speaker will digress from the main topic of his speech.
4. The club was making plans to induct new members.
5. It is not safe to exceed the posted speed limit.
6. The signs along the trail warned the hikers to proceed with caution.
7. The flood waters began to recede when the rain stopped.
8. Without a union, it is hard to find someone to intercede on the strikers' behalf.
9. The company was able to produce 25,000 video discs a day.
10. The composer wished to arrange and conduct his own music.

G SENTENCES FOR SPELLING EXERCISE

SEQUENCE 6-16

1. Trucks are used to transport produce from farm to supermarket.
2. The stockbroker was happy to report an increase in the stock's value.
3. A country must import products that it cannot produce.
4. Use an insecticide to repel insects.
5. Our country will deport illegal aliens who have committed a crime.
6. A strong desire to succeed seemed to impel the athlete to victory.
7. The wind was used to propel the glider over the mountains.
8. The directions did nothing but confuse the reader.
9. The store will not refund a customer's money without a receipt.
10. It is against the law to refuse someone a job based on race.

G SENTENCES FOR SPELLING EXERCISE

SEQUENCE 6-17

1. The jeweler was asked to inscribe initials on the pocket watch.
2. The driver was asked to describe the accident to the policeman.
3. Families often subscribe to a daily newspaper.
4. A good secretary must be able to transcribe letters and reports.
5. When going on vacation, it is a good idea to reserve a hotel room.
6. We must all work together to conserve our natural resources.
7. Many hard-working employees deserve higher wages.
8. The Constitution was written to preserve individual freedom.
9. The foreman was asked to inspect the work on the construction site.
10. Always respect the rights of others.

G SENTENCES FOR SPELLING EXERCISE

SEQUENCE 6-18

1. Supermarkets provide food for the people in the neighborhood.
2. We must make provision for the poor children in school to receive a hot lunch.
3. It's so nice to be in the country and inhale the fresh air.
4. Those who conspire against their country are called traitors.
5. The man was about to expire due to old age.
6. The coach tried to inspire his team to victory.
7. In order to live, we must inhale oxygen and exhale carbon dioxide.
8. When the radio's volume is turned off, the sound is inaudible.
9. The audience was eager to meet the show's cast.
10. The auditorium will hold a maximum of 500 people.

G SENTENCES FOR SPELLING EXERCISE

SEQUENCE 6-19

1. School will convene promptly at 9:00 a.m.
2. Many teachers attend the annual education convention.
3. When the couple argued, the marriage counselor was forced to intervene.
4. This is not a convenient time to take your call.
5. Parents hate to see their teenagers revert to childish behavior.
6. When fractions are divided, you must invert and multiply.
7. The candidate tried to pervert his opponent's image.
8. Xerox machines are used to duplicate important papers.
9. Due to an accident, police had to divert the freeway traffic.
10. The reporter tried to implicate the man in the crime.

G SENTENCES FOR SPELLING EXERCISE

SEQUENCE 6-20

1. When you bisect an angle, you cut it in half.
2. The sign cautioned that two roads will intersect one mile ahead.
3. Many girls do not like to dissect specimens in biology class.
4. The student tried to contradict what the teacher said.
5. Weathermen do not always predict the weather accurately.
6. We were instructed to indicate the correct answer by circling it.
7. Blinking and sneezing are reflexes.
8. A lead shield will deflect radioactive particles.
9. Children are often a reflection of their parents.
10. An intern must be willing to follow a flexible schedule.

G SENTENCES FOR SPELLING EXERCISE

SEQUENCE 6-21

1. The financial advisor tried to answer the man's questions.
2. The pianist wrote music for the piano.
3. The doctor set the boy's broken leg in a cast.
4. The sailor loved to spend his days on the sea.
5. The radio announcer said, "And now a word from our sponsor. . ."
6. The actress had trouble memorizing her lines.
7. The conductor arranged the music for the orchestra.
8. The waitress spilled soup on a customer.
9. The teacher gave the class homework every night.
10. The druggist filled the bottle with cough syrup.

G SENTENCES FOR SPELLING EXERCISE

SEQUENCE 6-22

1. Many people consider fine dining a form of entertainment.
2. The new housing development was still in the planning stages.
3. A bad sprain caused enlargement of the woman's ankle.
4. A great deal of concentration is necessary when playing chess.
5. The penetration of the bullet through the skin was painful.
6. The people resent government regulation of imports and exports.
7. The collision of the two trains injured many people.
8. The circumference of something is found by following a special formula.
9. The circumstances surrounding the accident is still a mystery.
10. A parent-teacher conference was called to discuss the student's progress.

G SENTENCES FOR SPELLING EXERCISE

SEQUENCE 6-23

1. Wise parents will assert authority over their children.
2. The simplicity of the dress made it a very popular style.
3. Given the opportunity, I would like to visit Europe.
4. The crack in the cement indicates a weakness in the sidewalk.
5. The slowness of the airlines make customers angry.
6. The smoothness of the slope made the skiing pleasant.
7. Running very fast can cause shortness of breath.
8. The previous owner of the car took good care of it.
9. When buying anything, it is best to be a cautious shopper.
10. The wedding was a wondrous affair.

G SENTENCES FOR SPELLING EXERCISE

SEQUENCE 6-24

1. The man waited for the bank's approval of his loan.
2. The files were stored in a vertical filing cabinet.
3. The horizontal lines on the chart were crooked.
4. The car started easily, even though it was extremely cold outside.
5. The rides at Disneyland are cleverly designed.
6. People who are hurt in car accidents must be moved carefully.
7. The little girl slammed the door angrily.
8. The soldier approached his adversary with caution.
9. A book review contains a short summary of a book.
10. Planetary maps show us the position of the planets.

G SENTENCES FOR SPELLING EXERCISE

SEQUENCE 6-25

1. Defective brakes failed to stop the car at the red light.
2. Primitive man discovered how to use fire to make his life easier.
3. The attractive model won the beauty pageant.
4. The witness provided a descriptive report of the accident.
5. Scientists classify things as either animal, vegetable, or mineral.
6. Americans must modify their use of gas to conserve resources.
7. You must magnify a tiny atom in order to see it.
8. The children in the neighborhood wanted to organize a baseball team.
9. The class wanted to dramatize the story for their parents.
10. Only a structural engineer can authorize changes to a building's structure.

G SENTENCES FOR SPELLING EXERCISE

SEQUENCE 6-26

1. The argument between the brothers was aimless.
2. The diamond was found to be flawless.
3. A country with no government would be lawless.
4. The policeman's bullet penetrated the man's leg.
5. The little girl had a ringlet in the middle of her forehead.
6. Another name for a baby pig is a piglet.
7. A ballerina must be very graceful on her feet.
8. Christmas is a joyful time of year.
9. Children should be taught to be respectful toward their elders.
10. The coach was hopeful that his team would win the World Series.

G SENTENCES FOR SPELLING EXERCISE

SEQUENCE 6-27

1. The steel beam's light weight was rejected by the engineer.
2. After losing her kitten, the little girl was dejected.
3. The sick child was admitted to the hospital.
4. An observatory is where astronomers study the stars through a telescope.
5. The scientist performed many experiments in his laboratory.
6. Most of the townspeople worked in the shoe factory.
7. Consult the museum's directory to get the curator's telephone extension.
8. The decorator helped the woman choose furniture and drapes for her home.
9. The fuel indicator showed that the car was almost out of gas.
10. Car dealerships often sell demonstrator models for lower prices.

G SENTENCES FOR SPELLING EXERCISE

SEQUENCE 6-28

1. Acreage on a lakefront costs a great deal of money.
2. A large percentage of the class did not pass the math test.
3. The army looks for men who possess courage.
4. A multitude of people attend the State Fair each year.
5. The magnitude of the disaster was impossible to measure.
6. The airplane reached an altitude of 30,000 feet.
7. The hiker had frostbite from exposure to the cold.
8. Old bones will fracture more readily than young bones.
9. Dinosaurs were discussed in a lecture by the paleontologist.
10. The manufacture of home appliances is an important industry.

G SENTENCES FOR SPELLING EXERCISE

SEQUENCE 6-29

1. The candidate hoped to win the Presidential election.
2. Many people were asked to participate in the homecoming celebration.
3. The rancher was forced to isolate the sick cow from the rest of the herd.
4. The new X-ray machine was a small, portable unit.
5. Meat is very perishable and must be kept refrigerated.
6. Children can be very manageable if they have strict parents.
7. If the boy did not get what he wanted, he was very disagreeable.
8. The painting was a classic example of modern art.
9. A household pet is a domestic animal.
10. The movie had a fantastic effect produced by the sound system.

G SENTENCES FOR SPELLING EXERCISE

SEQUENCE 6-30

1. The politician made known his intention to run for President.
2. We called an electrician to install new lights in the living room.
3. The beautician styled the bride's hair beautifully.
4. A pediatrician is a doctor who takes care of young children.
5. The machine's mechanism was broken, so the machine would not work.
6. Finding fault with others is called criticism.
7. Capitalism allows individuals to own property.
8. When people are feverish, their body temperature rises.
9. At times, adults act in childish ways.
10. If you love someone, you cherish that person.

ANSWER KEY

Sequences 6-1 to 6-3

SEQUENCE 6-1

B (page 2)

1. a, b
2. a
3. b
4. b
5. b

C (page 3)

1. exit, c
2. describe, c
3. subtract, b
4. except, b
5. descend, c

D (page 4)

1. deposit
2. subdivision
3. derive
4. except
5. exhaust

E (page 4)

1. exit
2. describe
3. derives
4. subtract
5. exhaust

SEQUENCE 6-2

B (page 6)

1. b
2. b
3. a
4. b
5. b

C (page 7)

1. uncertain, a
2. uncommon, b
3. independent, b
4. nonsense, c
5. unusual, b

D (page 8)

1. unconscious
2. invisible
3. nonfiction
4. uncertain
5. independent

E (page 8)

1. uncommon
2. nonfiction
3. unusual
4. nonliving
5. nonsense

SEQUENCE 6-3

B (page 10)

1. a
2. b
3. b
4. a
5. b

C (page 11)

1. circumstance, a
2. progress, a
3. percolate, a
4. perceive, a
5. project, c

D (page 12)

1. circumference
2. perceive
3. protect
4. progress
5. circumstances

E (page 12)

1. perceive
2. circumnavigate
3. progress
4. perform
5. percolate

ANSWER KEY

Sequences 6-4 to 6-6

SEQUENCE 6-4

B (page 14)

1. a, b
2. a
3. a
4. a
5. b

C (page 15)

1. postpone, c
2. prevent, b
3. rebuilt, c
4. reflect, c
5. precede, a

D (page 16)

1. predict
2. prevent
3. postscript
4. precede
5. postpone

E (page 16)

1. precede
2. postpone
3. prevent
4. reflected
5. rebuilt

SEQUENCE 6-5

B (page 18)

1. a
2. b
3. a, b
4. a
5. b

C (page 19)

1. biennial, b
2. biplane, b
3. monologue, c
4. unison, b
5. university, a

D (page 20)

1. bicycle
2. monologue
3. monotonous
4. unison
5. biennial

E (page 20)

1. monoplanes
2. United States
3. bicycle
4. university
5. monotonous

SEQUENCE 6-6

B (page 22)

1. a, b
2. b
3. b
4. b
5. b

C (page 23)

1. supermarket, c
2. multiform, b
3. semiautomatic, b
4. multitude, c
5. semicircle, c

D (page 24)

1. superior
2. multiple
3. semiautomatic
4. unskilled
5. semicircle

E (page 24)

1. semiskilled
2. multiple
3. superior
4. multitude
5. semiannually

ANSWER KEY

Sequences 6-7 to 6-9

SEQUENCE 6-7

B (page 26)

1. b
2. b
3. a, b
4. a, b
5. a

C (page 27)

1. antidote, a
2. antonym, b
3. counteract, c
4. contradict, a
5. contraband, a

D (page 28)

1. antidote
2. antonym
3. counteract
4. counterplot
5. contraband

E (page 28)

1. counteract
2. antonym
3. contradict
4. counteract
5. antipathy

SEQUENCE 6-8

B (page 30)

1. b
2. a
3. a
4. b
5. b

C (page 31)

1. compress, b
2. interplanetary, c
3. synonym, b
4. symphony, a
5. international, b

D (page 32)

1. synonym
2. sympathy
3. international
4. compete
5. interplanetary

E (page 32)

1. sympathy
2. compare
3. interstate
4. synonym
5. compete

SEQUENCE 6-9

B (page 34)

1. a
2. b
3. a
4. a
5. b

C (page 35)

1. epidermis, c
2. enclose, b
3. envelop, a
4. endanger, c
5. encircle, c

D (page 36)

1. epidermis
2. intramural
3. epidemic
4. enclose
5. engrave

E (page 36)

1. intrastate
2. intravenous
3. engrave
4. endanger
5. enclose

ANSWER KEY

Sequences 6-10 to 6-12

SEQUENCE 6-10

B (page 38)

1. a
2. b
3. a, b
4. b
5. a

C (page 39)

1. microbe, c
2. microphone, c
3. telephone, c
4. television, a
5. Microwaves, c

D (page 40)

1. microbe
2. magnified
3. magnificent
4. microscope
5. telephone

E (page 40)

1. microwave
2. telegraph
3. telepathy
4. television
5. microphone

SEQUENCE 6-11

B (page 42)

1. a
2. b
3. a
4. a
5. a

C (page 43)

1. submit, a
2. retract, b
3. permit, b
4. commit, a
5. reject, c

D (page 44)

1. admit
2. reject
3. commit
4. remit
5. subtract

E (page 44)

1. permit
2. inject
3. submit
4. detract
5. retract

SEQUENCE 6-12

B (page 46)

1. a, b
2. a
3. b
4. b
5. a

C (page 47)

1. depend, b
2. expend, a
3. exclude, a
4. depend, a
5. include, a

D (page 48)

1. manufacture
2. factual
3. appendix
4. conclude
5. depend

E (page 48)

1. expend
2. factory
3. suspend
4. conclude
5. exclude

ANSWER KEY

Sequences 6-13 to 6-15

SEQUENCE 6-13

B (page 50)

1. b
2. b
3. b
4. b
5. a

C (page 51)

1. position, b
2. proposition, c
3. evolve, b
4. solvent, b
5. solution, c

D (page 52)

1. proposition
2. resolve
3. revolve
4. disposition
5. position

E (page 52)

1. deposit
2. involve
3. evolve
4. proposition
5. dissolve

SEQUENCE 6-14

B (page 54)

1. b
2. b
3. a
4. b
5. b

C (page 55)

1. obtain, b
2. emotion, c
3. prelude, b
4. delude, b
5. remove, b

D (page 56)

1. retain
2. postlude
3. emotion
4. exclude
5. demote

E (page 56)

1. retain
2. prelude
3. interlude
4. delude
5. obtain

SEQUENCE 6-15

B (page 58)

1. a
2. b
3. b
4. b
5. b

C (page 59)

1. progress, b
2. digress, c
3. produce, a
4. recede, c
5. exceed, b

D (page 60)

1. exceed
2. intercede
3. induct
4. regress
5. progress

E (page 60)

1. digress
2. exceed
3. induct
4. produce
5. regress

ANSWER KEY

Sequences 6-16 to 6-18

SEQUENCE 6-16

B (page 62)

1. a
2. a
3. b
4. b
5. b

C (page 63)

1. refund, b
2. report, b.
3. impel, c
4. refuse, a
5. propel, b

D (page 64)

1. transport
2. import
3. repel
4. impel
5. refuse

E (page 64)

1. propel
2. refund
3. confuse
4. deport
5. import

SEQUENCE 6-17

B (page 66)

1. b
2. a
3. b
4. b
5. a

C (page 67)

1. conserve, b
2. deserve, c
3. preserve, a
4. inspect, c
5. respect, a

D (page 68)

1. respect
2. inscribe
3. conserve
4. transcribe
5. preserve

E (page 68)

1. describe
2. subscribe
3. conserve
4. reserve
5. deserve

SEQUENCE 6-18

B (page 70)

1. b
2. a
3. a
4. b
5. b

C (page 71)

1. exhale, b
2. inaudible, a
3. audience, b
4. auditorium, b
5. provide, b

D (page 72)

1. expire
2. inhale
3. exhale
4. provide
5. inaudible

E (page 72)

1. provision
2. conspire
3. auditorium
4. inspire
5. audience

ANSWER KEY

Sequences 6-19 to 6-21

SEQUENCE 6-19

B (page 74)

1. a, b
2. a
3. a
4. a
5. a

C (page 75)

1. convene, c
2. intervene, b
3. revert, a
4. pervert, c
5. implicate, a

D (page 76)

1. convene
2. convention
3. convenient
4. divert
5. duplicate

E (page 76)

1. invert
2. revert
3. duplicate
4. intervene
5. implicate

SEQUENCE 6-20

B (page 78)

1. b
2. a
3. a
4. b
5. a

C (page 79)

1. dissect, a
2. reflection, b
3. contradict, b
4. flexible, a
5. indicate, c

D (page 80)

1. intersect
2. flexible
3. contradict
4. indicate
5. predict

E (page 80)

1. bisect
2. reflexes
3. reflect
4. predict
5. dissect

SEQUENCE 6-21

B (page 82)

1. a
2. b
3. a, b
4. b
5. a

C (page 83)

1. actress, c
2. advisor, c
3. pianist, a
4. druggist, b
5. announcer, a

D (page 84)

1. doctor
2. pianist
3. conductor
4. teacher
5. advisor

E (page 84)

1. actress
2. doctor
3. sailor
4. announcer
5. druggist

ANSWER KEY

Sequences 6-22 to 6-24

SEQUENCE 6-22

B (page 86)

1. b
2. a
3. a
4. b
5. b

C (page 87)

1. collision, b
2. circumference, c
3. circumstance, c
4. regulation, c
5. conference, a

D (page 88)

1. entertainment
2. development
3. collision
4. enlargement
5. concentration

E (page 88)

1. penetration
2. collision
3. circumference
4. regulation
5. entertainment

SEQUENCE 6-23

B (page 90)

1. b
2. a
3. a
4. b
5. b

C (page 91)

1. smoothness, b
2. shortness, c
3. previous, b
4. wondrous, a
5. cautious, a

D (page 92)

1. authority
2. opportunity
3. wondrous
4. weakness
5. cautious

E (page 92)

1. previous
2. smoothness
3. cautious
4. simplicity
5. slowness

SEQUENCE 6-24

B (page 94)

1. a
2. b
3. b
4. a
5. a

C (page 95)

1. carefully, a
2. adversary, b
3. planetary, b
4. summary, a
5. angrily, c

D (page 96)

1. easily
2. summary
3. approval
4. adversary
5. cleverly

E (page 96)

1. vertical
2. carefully
3. approval
4. planetary
5. horizontal

ANSWER KEY

Sequences 6-25 to 6-27

SEQUENCE 6-25

B (page 98)

1. b
2. a
3. b
4. a
5. a

C (page 99)

1. descriptive, c
2. classify, c
3. magnify, b
4. authorize, c
5. organize, c

D (page 100)

1. Primitive
2. classify
3. modify
4. dramatize
5. magnify

E (page 100)

1. defective
2. classify
3. attractive
4. organize
5. modify

SEQUENCE 6-26

B (page 102)

1. b
2. b
3. b
4. b
5. a

C (page 103)

1. flawless, c
2. piglet, c
3. graceful, b
4. bullet, a
5. hopeful, c

D (page 104)

1. joyful
2. flawless
3. aimless
4. respectful
5. ringlet

E (page 104)

1. lawless
2. flawless
3. hopeful
4. bullet
5. graceful

SEQUENCE 6-27

B (page 106)

1. a
2. b
3. a
4. b
5. b

C (page 107)

1. rejected, b
2. laboratory, c
3. directory, c
4. demonstrator, a
5. admitted, b

D (page 108)

1. observatory
2. directory
3. factory
4. indicator
5. laboratory

E (page 108)

1. dejected
2. laboratory
3. factory
4. decorator
5. demonstrator

ANSWER KEY

Sequences 6-28 to 6-30

SEQUENCE 6-28

B (page 110)

1. b
2. a
3. a
4. a
5. a

C (page 111)

1. altitude, a
2. exposure, b
3. fracture, c
4. manufacture, b
5. lecture, b

D (page 112)

1. exposure
2. acreage
3. altitude
4. fracture
5. magnitude

E (page 112)

1. multitude
2. courage
3. lecture
4. manufacture
5. percentage

SEQUENCE 6-29

B (page 114)

1. a
2. b
3. b
4. a
5. a

C (page 115)

1. manageable, a
2. classic, c
3. domestic, b
4. disagreeable, a
5. fantastic, c

D (page 116)

1. disagreeable
2. perishable
3. candidate
4. participate
5. classic

E (page 117)

1. isolate
2. fantastic
3. portable
4. classic
5. manageable

SEQUENCE 6-30

B (page 118)

1. a, b
2. b
3. a
4. b
5. b

C (page 119)

1. criticism, b
2. feverish, b
3. cherish, c
4. capitalism, a
5. childish, a

D (page 120)

1. mechanism
2. politician
3. feverish
4. electrician
5. criticism

E (page 120)

1. beautician
2. childish
3. capitalism
4. pediatrician
5. cherish

PROGRESS CHART

SCORE 20 POINTS FOR EACH CORRECT ANSWER IN EXERCISES D AND E.
SCORE 10 POINTS FOR EACH CORRECT ANSWER IN EXERCISE G.

(EXAMPLE)

SEQUENCE NUMBER	SEQUENCE SECTION SCORE D	E	G	PAGE NUMBER	DATE
6-1	80			4	September 12, 2004
		100		4	September 12, 2004
			90		September 15, 2004

SEQUENCE NUMBER	SEQUENCE SECTION SCORE D	E	G	PAGE NUMBER	DATE
6-1					
6-2					
6-3					

SEQUENCE NUMBER	SEQUENCE SECTION SCORE D	E	G	PAGE NUMBER	DATE
6-4					
6-5					
6-6					
6-7					
6-8					
6-9					
6-10					
6-11					

SEQUENCE NUMBER	SEQUENCE SECTION SCORE			PAGE NUMBER	DATE
	D	E	G		
6-12					
6-13					
6-14					
6-15					
6-16					
6-17					
6-18					
6-19					

SEQUENCE NUMBER	SEQUENCE SECTION SCORE D	E	G	PAGE NUMBER	DATE
6-20					
6-21					
6-22					
6-23					
6-24					
6-25					
6-26					
6-27					

SEQUENCE NUMBER	SEQUENCE SECTION SCORE D	E	G	PAGE NUMBER	DATE
6-28					
6-29					
6-30					